PRACT

Pruning

*KEEP YOUR SHRUBS AND
TREES IN GOOD SHAPE*

DONALD FARTHING

foulsham

LONDON · NEW YORK · TORONTO · SYDNEY

W. FOULSHAM & COMPANY LIMITED
Yeovil Road, SLOUGH, Berkshire SL1 4JH

ISBN 0-572-01645-X
© W. Foulsham & Co. Ltd. 1991

Acknowledgements
Illustrations: GUY FARTHING R.I.B.A., Dip L.Arch.
          assisted by William Tucker R.I.B.A.,
          A.I.L.A.

Printed in Great Britain by
St Edmundsbury Press, Bury St Edmunds, Suffolk

Contents

Introduction

Of all the skills a gardener has to learn, pruning is the one that seems to cause most confusion and bewilderment. Armed with saw or secateurs, he goes out with vague ideas of "cutting back"—and with the hope rather than the belief that to do so will bring about a magical profusion of bloom and fruit. Well, it can happen. But hit-or-miss methods usually do more harm than good.

Much can be learned by watching an expert at work over a period of time, though even then his methods may not at first be understood. Many attempts have been made to clear the fog of misunderstanding in books and treatises on pruning but, with some exceptions, many tend to bog the reader down in technicalities and an excess of detail. The major difficulty in instructing by the written word is that there can be no parade ground drills, no cut-and-dried methods. For plants—like people—do not grow in the same way nor behave in the same way. But they can usually be relied on to re-act alike, in accordance with certain BIOLOGICAL GUIDELINES. *Within these guidelines—there are ten of them—lies the key to successful pruning.*

Learn them thoroughly, so that they are always at your finger tips, and any terrors or uncertainties attached to pruning will fall away.

Here they are:-

1. Every plant strives to reproduce itself as a whole by seed, suckers or other means; and seeks to replace any branch or stem it is deprived of.

2. Except when a plant is dormant, sap rises to the top of every shoot, and the topmost bud of a shortened

stem is the one that will "break" (burst into growth) first.

3. The removal of wood above a growth bud or shoot diverts energy into that bud or shoot: the harder the pruning the stronger the reaction.

4. Pruning delays flowering (and therefore fruiting) while the new shoots build or re-build a framework.

5. Young growth has more vigour than old, and can be expected to be more productive.

6. Reducing the amount of growth *lowers* the number of flowers and fruits, but *heightens* the quality.

7. Admitting light and air to the centre of a tree or shrub (unless it is of naturally "tight" shape) improves health—and therefore vigour—and the production of flower buds.

8. Dead, diseased or damaged wood endangers health.

9. Branches growing horizontally or diagonally produce more flowering shoots than vertical ones, and therefore more fruit.

10. Pruning deprives a plant of some of its food (manufactured through the leaves), and this must be replaced by feeding the roots.

With these basic facts as a rock-steady, reliable platform for your pruning operations, you will be able to follow with ease the special techniques relating to fruit trees and bushes, roses, shrubs of different habit, climbers and hedges. In describing them, I shall use the simplest language I can, and you will find explicit diagrams to make the methods doubly clear. Correct timing is important, but will present no difficulty once you know the *habit* of your tree or shrub. This information is contained in the easy reference A—Z section which forms the second part of this book, together with concise pruning directions.

A WORD ABOUT WORDS . . .

To make sure that you understand what I am going to talk about, I would ask you (with apologies to experienced gardeners) to run through the following list which explains the terms it is most convenient to use.

BASAL SHOOT—One arising at, or close to, ground level.

CALLUS—Corky tissue that grows over and heals a wound.

CORDON—A single-stemmed fruit bush.

DEAD HEADING—Removal of spent flowers.

DECIDUOUS—Shedding leaves in autumn.

DEHORNING—Removing old or large branches to reduce the height of a tree.

DIE-BACK—The decay and death, progressively from the top, of a branch, stems, or shoot.

DORMANT—Resting.

ESPALIER—A tree (usually fruiting) grown with its branches trained out horizontally from a central stem.

EVERGREEN—A plant which retains its leaves throughout the year.

EXTENSION GROWTH—Growth from a terminal bud.

FAN—A tree or shrub (usually fruiting) trained fanwise from a short central stem against a wall or other support.

FEATHERS—Side shoots arising from the stem of a maiden (first year) tree.

FRUIT BUD—One capable of flowering and fruiting, as compared with a growth bud (see below).

GROWING POINT—The bud at the end of a shoot.

GROWTH BUD—A bud capable of producing a shoot, as against a fruit bud.

LATERAL—A side-shoot.

LEADER—A main stem, or extension of a branch.

LEG—A bare stem, devoid of side-shoots.

MAIDEN—A single stem of one season's growth following grafting.

PINCHING OUT—Removing a growing point with the fingers.

POLLARDING—Cutting back bare branches severely to the top of the trunk, or a restricted framework of branches.

PYRAMID—A fruit tree trained in a roughly conical shape.

REPLACEMENT—A stem used to replace an older one.

REVERSION—The term used when a sport (see below) or variegation changes back to its original form.

RIPE WOOD—Growth that has matured from its early soft, sappy condition.

ROOTSTOCK—The shortened part of a parent plant on which a different plant, usually a variety, is grafted.

SCION—The part of a plant grafted on a rootstock.

SHOOT—A newly emerged stem.

SNAG—A 'hat peg' or stub left when a branch is not cut close enough to the trunk or parent branch.

SPORT—A plant that shows distinctive characteristics compared with its normal form.

SPUR—A number of fruit buds clustering near a stem or branch.

SPUR-BEARING—A tree or shrub that produces its flowers/fruit on spurs.

STANDARD—A tree with a bare stem below its branch system (6—7 ft normally, but 4ft 6in for roses).

STOLON—A creeping stem, usually underground.

STOOL—A plant from the crown of which a number of shoots springs annually, either naturally or when induced by pruning.

STOPPING—The removal of a growing point to induce side-shoots.

SUB-LATERAL—A side-shoot arising from a lateral.

SUCKER—A shoot arising from a root, or the rootstock of a grafted plant.

TAP ROOT—Central vertical root.

TERMINAL BUD—A bud at the end of a shoot or stem.

TIP BEARER—A fruit tree that bears some of its fruit, especially in early years, on the ends of shoots rather than on spurs.

WATER SHOOTS—Sappy growths arising from the trunk, or near the base of the main branches, of a tree or shrub, especially around a wound.

WOOD—Simply, ripened growth: a term widely used when discussing pruning.

CHAPTER ONE

Why Prune at All?

Is pruning really necessary? You may well wonder when you take a walk in the country and see magnificent trees growing naturally, with perfect shape and balance.

But modern man wants flowers and fruit in his garden, which he can reach and enjoy by walking only a few paces. He wants bigger flowers, richer colours, larger fruit of better flavour. To have all these he has to divert the natural energy of the plant into producing the kind of flowers or fruit he desires, or persuading a tree or bush to grow to the size and shape he wants, or emphasising desirable characteristics.

All this can be done with pruning. Not careless, haphazard pruning, which can easily do more harm than good, but thoughtful pruning—based on those ten BIOLOGICAL GUIDELINES. Keeping them in mind, you can go out with saw or secateurs with the same confidence as a surgeon uses his scalpel. But you don't need the years of training a surgeon has to undergo: just the plain knowledge of the way a plant grows and the way it will re-act to your surgery. This book will tell you exactly what to do—whether it be fruit tree, flowering shrub, or house plant—but there's no better way of impressing this guidance on your mind than by *observing*.

Look closely at your subject both when it is growing (normally during spring and summer) and when it is dormant and resting (in winter). When you prune, say, a rose in March, examine it in May and see how it is behaving as a direct result of that pruning: how many buds have broken into life, in which direction they are growing, whether a flower bud is developing. Or inspect an apple shoot in winter and look for the flat, stem-hugging buds that will produce new shoots and the plumper, scalier buds that are fruit buds. Watch as these buds burst into blossom, notice how many fruits form, how many drop, how many form perfect fruits; and see what happens to the growth buds, how strongly (or weakly) they grow during the summer. Observation of this kind will complement the written word, and provide the finishing school to the basic instruction.

Now let's go into a little more detail. There are five major reasons for pruning, and these are:-
1. To maximise production of flowers and/or fruit;
2. To get the size and quality of flower or fruit you want;
3. To achieve or preserve a desired shape;
4. To limit size; and
5. To maintain health and vigour.

The last reason is the most important of all, for all the others depend on it. No tree or shrub can do its work properly—any more than a human being can—unless it is healthy and strong. So before any other pruning is done, damaged or diseased branches or shoots must be removed. This not only averts the danger of 'die-back' affecting the healthy wood below, and the menace of disease spores or pests that may be lurking in the unsound wood, but—by its disappearance—gives more room for healthy wood to develop.

Whether you are seeking beautiful flowers or fine fruit your aim must be to secure a balance between the production of new growth and the production of the flowers or fruit. Over-production of new, sappy growth will be at the expense of fruit. On the other hand, too many fruit buds at the expense of new, healthy growth will result in poorer fruit and gradually weaken the tree. The ideal is an exact balance between the two. The achievement of this balance is so important that I should like to explain it further. Every plant builds up a supply of energy to make it grow—energy to form and develop roots, stems, leaves, flowers, fruit. This energy derives from the roots, which—besides anchoring the plant—draw up food, in solution, from the soil; and from the leaves, which manufacture further food, converting it from light by means of the green chlorophyll in their tissues. Compare this energy, this power unit, with a car battery.

Now a plant has one aim in life, and that is to reproduce itself—usually by means of seed which, in some cases, is encased in edible fruit. So while it is young, the power in the plant's battery is poured into extending its root system and building up a framework of branches and shoots along which it can form its flowers and fruit. As the plant matures, so an increasing amount of energy is used in the production of these flowers and that fruit. Growth slows down until, with age, it almost ceases as the hard-worked battery strives to keep up the fruit-and-seed production. That's the normal pattern, just as it is in our own lives. But, as with human beings and motor cars, things can go wrong. To start with, the battery—although sound—can get run down. The reason (plant-wise) could be semi-starvation. Two possible causes: (1) lack of soil nutrients, or (2) lack of light, depressing the amount of food the leaves can manufacture. The remedies are obvious: manure or otherwise fertilise the soil, and increase the amount of light.

A third cause of run-down could be shortage of leaves resulting from hard pruning. The act of hard pruning will in itself stimulate vigorous new growth but while new shoots are forming the deficiency should be made good with compensating enrichment of the soil.

But even if the plant battery is in good shape, all may not be well. Too much energy may be going into the making of new growth, and not enough into the production of flowers and fruit: or vice versa. The root cause of this is usually an imbalance of nutrients in the soil—an excess of nitrogen can depress shoot production. But it is not always easy to get the proportions balanced. And this is where correct pruning has an important part to play.

Take the case of too much growth, not enough fruit. Hard pruning, as you have already learned, produces a strong reaction in terms of growth. So that's out: light pruning is sufficient, or none at all. In stubborn

10

cases you may need to curb growth in other ways—by root pruning or by bark ringing (these two methods are described on pages 16 to 18) and by allowing grass to grow beneath the tree to absorb excess nitrogen. Now suppose it's the other way round: too many fruit buds, yielding a lot of small fruit, and not enough healthy new shoots. The need is to stimulate growth—and that means hard pruning and plenty of feeding, both immediate and long-term. When growth is the prime need, the accent should be on nitrogen: when fruit, on potash. When all is settled down, both should be given annually, with phosphates every second or third year. A mulch of farm manure, if possible every autumn, will not only help to feed the soil over a long period, but will condition it physically too. So you will see that pruning should always go hand in hand with feeding.

A word about limiting size. Most trees and shrubs will submit—some more readily than others—to fairly severe pruning to keep them within desired limits. Most hedging plants, such as yew or privet, are trimmed regularly summer after summer and are none the worse for it. Certain shrubs, flowering on wood made in the same season, are cut almost to the ground each year and survive without complaint. But a handsome tree, growing naturally with perfect shape, can be ruined by lopping its branches. And a once beautiful and graceful shrub can become ugly and distorted from the attentions of saw or shears. I would sooner you got rid of an over-hacked tree or shrub than preserve it in an unattractive condition.

The real answer to the problem of size is, of course, to make sure you know the ultimate height and spread of anything you plant, and choose accordingly. Too many people have planted Atlantic cedars or weeping willows in their front gardens only to find that, after the first few years when they are a joy, they become an embarrassment—if not a danger to the house foundations—by their size. I am not going to say that it is impossible to reduce the size of a tree or shrub dramatically by careful pruning, but I do put in a plea to approach the problem from the other end: Plant only what you have room for!

11

CHAPTER TWO

The Right Tools – and How to Use Them

There can be no good pruning without good tools—tools that fit the job, tools that are well-designed and comfortable to use, tools that are really sharp. Blunt ones—any that fail to make a clean cut first time must be classed as blunt—will bruise or tear the shoot or branch, inviting the entry of disease spores or bacteria. This apart, your pruning will be a much more pleasurable job if you are using keen blades. One reads a lot about "the pruner's knife". It's true that a knife, in the hands of a skilled gardener, probably makes the best cut of all, but in the hands of most amateurs it can be a dangerous weapon. You will still need one to pare cuts made with a saw, or to repair accidental tearing, but for most pruning jobs, equip yourself with a well-made, efficient pair of secateurs. They will serve you well if you look after them.

There are two main types—the parrot-beak type (mostly not so "beak-like" as they used to be, but with the same action) and the anvil type, by which the cutting blade bites against a platform, with a slight rolling motion. If you can afford it, have a pair of each, for the beak type—in my view—are better for cutting soft growth, and the anvil type for tough, woody growth; though either will do both jobs adequately. A minor point, unconnected with pruning, is that the anvil type will cut non-taut string. Before buying secateurs, make sure they fit the hand comfortably, do not need too much pressure, and have an easy-to-use catch for keeping the secateurs in the closed position (it should be possible to flick it "on" or "off" with the thumb). If you have to pay a little more for secateurs that meet all these requirements,

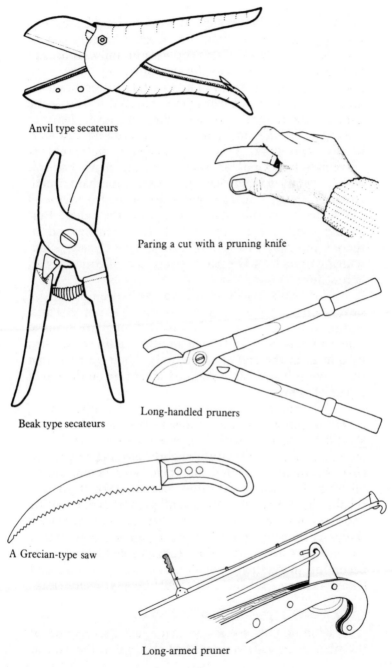

Anvil type secateurs

Paring a cut with a pruning knife

Beak type secateurs

Long-handled pruners

A Grecian-type saw

Long-armed pruner

13

don't begrudge the money. It's the one gardening tool you can't afford to skimp on. Good secateurs can be expected to cut woody stems up to ¾ in. thick. It doesn't pay to try to force them through anything bigger: you may easily damage them. The tool for cutting branches up to 1½ in. thick is a pair of long-handled pruners—the handles are roughly two feet long and give plenty of leverage. Stouter branches need a pruning saw—or, ideally, two saws. This is because you will probably encounter two kinds of wood—soft and hard. For soft wood, widely spaced teeth are better; for hard wood, close-set teeth. You can buy a double-edged saw with coarse teeth on one side and fine on the other. But, having used one to my cost, I don't recommend it: there's too much danger of damaging a closely neighbouring branch. A Grecian pruning saw, slightly curved, is best for all-round use.

For really big branches you will need a full-size saw, such as a bow saw. A useful, but not essential addition to your armoury is a pair of long-arm pruners (the arm may be 6—8 ft long and the blades are worked by a lever at the end of a long rod). Their virtue is that they save you a possibly perilous adventure on the top of a pair of steps.

All pruning tools must be kept absolutely clean, otherwise they can easily transmit disease. The blades should be cleaned, with fine emery paper if necessary, after use and wiped with a slightly oily rag to prevent rust. From time to time they may need honing on an oilstone. If you can't do this yourself, take them to a reliable hardware store for attention. For hedge cutting and the light trimming of some shrubs, a pair of garden shears is indispensable. Electric trimmers, both mains and cordless (these have tiny rechargeable batteries), are becoming increasingly popular, and are both time - and labour - saving. But they, too, must be kept really clean.

CUTTING—THE CORRECT WAY

Pruning cuts are always made just above a bud (if the plant is in leaf, you will find the bud in the axil, or junction of stem and leaf: so you prune just above the leaf, or pair of leaves). If the cut is made too high above the bud, the wood will die back to the point of the new shoot—and may damage that shoot. If the cut is too close to the bud, the flow of sap to the bud may be hindered and a poor shoot, or none at all, may result. There are several ways to make a pruning cut, but only one correct way. It must start immediately opposite the bud and slope up slightly to finish just above the bud (if there is a pair of buds, cut immediately above but, again, with a slight slope). One reason for the angle is to allow moisture to drain quickly off the wound—for a wound it is, until it heals. I'm not going to say that a clean cut directly across the stem and above the bud will not be adequate in most cases. But why not be 100 per cent sure of success? Make a habit of doing it the right way. When branches (or thick stems) are pruned, they must be cut close against the main branch (or stem). A snag or "hat peg"—portion of wood left projecting—is not only unsightly but liable to cause die-back damage.

Care must be taken when lopping a heavy branch. If you saw it through, it will tear the bark badly as it falls. So first make a cut an inch or two deep on the underside, about a foot away from the trunk or major branch. Then saw through from the top an inch or so on the outer side of the lower cut. The branch will then come away cleanly, or almost so. Finish the job by removing the

The right way to cut

snag, cutting it nearly, but not quite, flush with the parent wood. Cuts in wood more than an inch in diameter should always be sealed—within an hour if possible—to prevent disease spores entering. Lead (white) paint may be used, but this is conspicuous and it's well worth buying a proprietary sealant, such as Arbrex. Keep a supply always at hand.

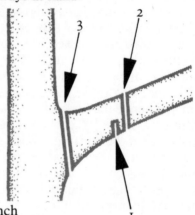

Removing a branch

Nature has her own way of healing a cut by forming corky tissue, called callus, over the wound. This is completed quickly when the cut is small (as when you prune the year-old growth of a rose) but can take many years in the case of a large wound (as when a tree branch is lopped). This does not matter—the important thing is to seal the cut quickly. Any rough edges around the wound should first be carefully pared smooth with a sharp knife. Finally always cut back into healthy wood. Your eye will tell you where it is safe to cut in most cases—but not always. If, having made a cut, you see a dark spot in the centre of the stem, contrasting with the colour of the other tissue, that's a sign that disease has spread down to that point. So cut lower until no such tell-tale spot is seen.

ROOT PRUNING

The practice of root pruning over-vigorous fruit trees—or, much more rarely, ornamental trees—is not so

16

common nowadays, when a variety of rootstocks is available to control size and vigour to required limits. But you may well have an established tree which would benefit. The effect of removing the outer roots is, of course, to limit the supply of nutrients being sent up and therefore to check the amount of top growth that is being made. To avoid too drastic a check, root pruning should normally be carried out in two stages—half the roots being cut one winter, half the next. This is the method:- Dig a trench about a foot wide and not less than 18 inches deep around the tree, just inside the outer branches. All thick branches are severed—a pruning saw or long-handled pruners are the best tools—but thin, fibrous ones are left. Where possible, cut cleanly against a thicker parent root—just as you would remove a top-growth branch—and if it is thicker than an inch, coat it with sealant. Fill in the removed soil, making sure that it is well worked down, leaving no air pockets. Finally, tread well down.

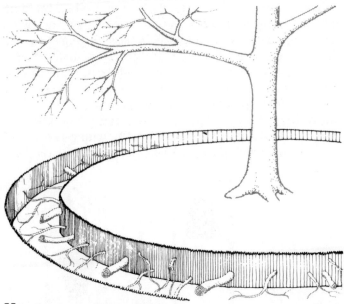

How to root-prune a tree

Another method of checking excessive growth when ordinary pruning methods fail is called bark ringing. This also has the effect of checking the supply of nutrients to the branches and therefore inhibiting growth. To remove a band of bark all the way round the trunk or branch of a tree would be to sign its death warrant. So, to allow the sap to continue to rise, though in a restricted way, a band of bark tissue is removed with a sharp knife—not more than half an inch wide—around half the circumference of the stem and repeated on the opposite side, but a couple of inches higher or lower. Seal the wounds with adhesive tape. The effect of bark ringing— most easily done in late spring—is to promote the formation of fruit buds above the ring, and to slow new growth. It works well with apples, pears, and vines, but should not be practised with stone fruits, which are likely to exude gum when so cut.

NOTCHING AND NICKING

You should know two ways of controlling the behaviour of a bud—particularly useful when building up the framework of a young tree. They are called notching and nicking, and—as in bark ringing—it is the flow of sap that is affected. Cut a notch—a small triangle of bark—just above a bud and it will be stimulated into growth. Cut a nick, in the same way, just below a bud and its development will be weakened, if not halted altogether. Young branches often carry a number of dormant buds near their base, and notching is a useful way of waking them up. Again, late spring is the best time.

a) Notching.
b) Nicking

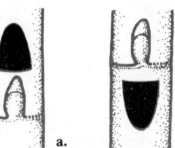

a.   b.

CHAPTER THREE

Creating a Beautiful Tree

Ornamental trees are an important feature in any garden, even the smallest, lending it height, beauty, and all-year-round interest. Because they are likely to be in key positions, the aim must be to keep them in good health, well clothed, and looking as attractive as possible. And that will almost certainly involve a degree of pruning. For although a tree will normally develop according to its natural habit—and it would be foolish to interfere with that—it often needs a reminder or a little guidance. Severe surgery should never be necessary, especially to limit size, for this means that the tree was ill-chosen in the first place. When deciding on a tree—or shrub, or a plant of any kind—always find out just how tall and how spreading it is going to become. Be sure it is right for the site.

A young tree bought at a nursery or garden centre will have a strong leading stem and a number of short side branches, sometimes called feathers. Some will be too low on the trunk to be retained, but don't remove too many at once—just gradually over two or three years, reducing the rest to three buds. If the tree is to be a standard (growing, say, in the lawn) all side branches up to a height of about 7 ft should eventually be removed. This will enable you to walk, and mow, under it without interference. Meanwhile the head of branches will be forming, and your object should be to encourage it into as shapely a form as you can.

Cut out completely any branches that threaten to cross or rub against others and as always—except for most conifers and fastigiate (very upright) trees—keep the centre of the tree open to admit light and air

(Guideline 7). Sometimes a second strong central leader will form as a rival to the main one. To allow it to grow on would not only hinder the tree's development, but create an inherent weakness. Water and decaying matter is apt to collect in the junction of two such stems and start a rotting process which, in the end, may cause one of the two branches to collapse. So, at an early stage, choose the stronger or better placed of the two rivals and eliminate the other. Once a tree is well established and growing steadily, little or no pruning should be necessary. Rely on the in-bred instinct of the species to form a shapely, handsome head. Only when it steps out of line with wayward growth, or when a branch becomes diseased or damaged, should surgery be necessary.

Deciduous trees should generally be pruned when they are leafless and the sap has ceased to flow: in other words, when they are resting. The safest period is between late autumn and late winter. Pruning a tree when it is in leaf not only gives it a check, mild or violent according to the amount of leafage lost, but is more difficult to carry out. Some families, including birch, maple and walnut, tend to bleed from the wounds if cut in late winter or early spring, and should therefore be pruned towards the end of the year. Ornamental plums and cherries—like the fruiting kinds—often produce gum when the branches are cut. Fortunately little pruning should be necessary, but if it is, do it soon after midsummer, when the wounds will heal quickest. In any case, remember to apply a sealant, which will check gumming, if not stop it entirely.

Conifers, on the whole, have a tidy, symmetrical habit of growth and rarely need pruning unless their owner wants to trim them in a certain way, as when forming a hedge. Few conifers dislike such mild pruning, but most resent hard cutting back, and some—like cupressus macrocarpa—may succumb to it. General trimming should be done in summer—not later, or the young shoots resulting may be damaged by frost. Other evergreens are best pruned in spring—unless, of course, they are about to flower—as new growth begins. Flowering kinds should be pruned immediately after the flowers fade. Large-leafed evergreens, such as bay, should always be pruned with secateurs, not shears, which will slice the leaves and turn the edges brown.

What are you to do if you are saddled with a tree, perhaps planted by some previous owner, that has outgrown its space in the garden and may be encroaching on the house or interfering with a view? Wholesale and immediate lopping must be avoided: not only does this damage the health of the tree, but the result will inevitably be unsightly. So spread the work over at least two years. Think hard about how the tree will look if you remove this branch or that: the process cannot be reversed and too many badly mutilated trees are seen. If possible—and it generally is—a large branch should be reduced as far as a healthy sub-branch, growing in an acceptable direction. Never leave an unsightly stump. If the tree is not yet fully mature, and is healthy, hard cutting back will inevitably stimulate vigorous new growth, and you may well have to repeat the process after a few years.

A common method of controlling a tree's height and spread is by pollarding, producing "mop head" growth. This involves cutting all the annual growth very close to the trunk or major branches in late winter.

A word of warning . . . although it is easy enough to hire a powered saw, which enormously eases and speeds the work of removing branches (not to mention the job of sawing them up into logs), the amateur operator should be quite sure how to use it. He should also realise the great weight of large branches. Their fall may not only damage other parts of the tree, but cause injury to the user or by-standers. The weight can be taken by a rope slung over a high limb or cleft, and lowered gradually, but unless you are quite confident, I strongly advise calling in a qualified tree surgeon for any major work.

CHAPTER FOUR

How to Prune Shrubs

While most shrubs, once safely established, are quite capable of looking after themselves and producing the flowers, foliage and berries expected of them, they will not necessarily do it in the way you want. Which is, of course, to provide an attractive, long-lasting display of maximum quality. To achieve that, the majority need care and guidance, with pruning that may be regular or just occasional.

The prime reason for pruning a shrub is to ensure its health, for—like an athlete—it cannot succeed without good lungs, sound limbs, and latent vigour. Next we want to help it to fit gracefully the position we have chosen for it—a solo site, perhaps, in the lawn; as a contrast or complement to an adjacent shrub or tree (never neglect to consider the effect of a new arrival on its neighbours, and vice versa); on a bank, beside a pool, or against a wall. Shape is important, too, but the shrub should always look natural—except when it is the subject of a hedge or a piece of topiary. And finally, sensible pruning enables a shrub to show off its special characteristics to best advantage—whether they be fine flowers, striking foliage, richly coloured berries or bark.

If you already have established shrubs in your garden, some of them perhaps many years old, can they be improved by pruning? Almost certainly. First, there will probably be a good deal of dead wood; and the time to get rid of this, if the shrubs are deciduous, is soon after they break into leaf in spring, when you can easily distinguish the dead wood from the living. Next, the branches or stems are likely to be overcrowded, especially in the centre. Cut out the oldest wood, as low down as you can without spoiling the appearance of the bush. If you feel the shrub is getting too large, or unbalanced, prune some of the longest branches back to a younger replacement branch, which should not be less than half the diameter of the one you are removing. If major surgery is necessary, it's usually wise to spread it over two years, although some shrubs will not object to a single drastic operation (See the Alphabetical List). Apart from cutting out dead wood, the pruning of deciduous shrubs is usually carried out in the dormant period. Avoid periods of hard frost.

Now let's turn to the purchase and treatment of young shrubs. The growth of garden centres in recent years has greatly popularised the sale of container-grown plants. The reasons are plain: you can see the plant you are buying (if you are lucky you may find your intended purchase in flower or fruit) and you can take it home and plant it at any time of the year, in open weather. Being able to inspect your shrub—instead of buying blind a bare-root specimen from a nursery, good as it may be—enables you to choose one that is sturdy (not thin or leggy) with foliage of good colour (not pale or yellowing) and with 3—5 strong well-balanced stems.

Does a shrub need any pruning after you have planted it? Certainly remove any damaged growth, and perhaps tip back the leading stems, but generally allow it one season to become established. Your aim then must be to encourage the shrub to build up a strong framework. Slow-growing shrubs can normally be relied on to look after themselves, and little pruning is necessary. The faster growers usually benefit from fairly hard pruning of the leading stems to maintain their vigour and cause laterals to develop, so encouraging a bushy habit. These laterals, if they grow long, can themselves be shortened the following pruning season. You may, by this formative pruning, lose early flowers you would otherwise have been able to enjoy, but the sacrifice is worth while if it results in a stonger, shapelier, free flowering shrub for future years.

The plant you buy will be growing either on its own

roots (as, for instance, a hydrangea) or grafted, or budded, on a rootstock (as with a hybrid tea rose). It's important to know which—and if you don't you can usually tell by checking the existence of a union, the thickened part of the stem, normally just above soil level, where the scion was joined to the rootstock. If there is a union, and therefore a rootstock, watch out for sappy growths arising from *below* the union called suckers. These, if uncurbed, will put in a take-over bid for the grafted top growth, starve it out, and score a total victory. But the victory is a defeat for the gardener, and these suckers must be rigorously removed as they appear. How do you know that they are part of the stock and not the desired plant? One way is to compare their leaves with those on shoots higher up the shrub. A surer way is to trace the growth back to its source. If it arises from a point below the union, it is a sucker and must go: if above, it is part of the desired plant. A few garden shrubs growing on their own roots have a naturally suckering habit, and as many suckers as are needed should therefore be retained.

"When should I prune this shrub or that?" is a question you may well ask. No need to inquire if one vital fact is learned about the shrub: *Does it flower on growth made in the same season?—OR—Does it flower on growth made the previous year?* You can answer this question easily enough for yourself if you study the behaviour of the shrub through twelve consecutive months. But you could find this inconvenient. So, for your guidance, you will find the best time to prune a particular shrub in the Alphabetical List (pages 79—128). This will make a good, quick reference point as well as helping inexperienced gardeners to learn more about their shrubs before buying them, or without waiting to observe them for a full year.

Let's see why a shrub's flowering habit determines when it should be pruned. The next section examines the types of shrub in more detail.

FLOWERING ON THE CURRENT SEASON'S GROWTH

Shrubs in this category are pruned early in the year to give them time to build up their flowering shoots. Some develop quicker than others. A bush rose pruned in spring takes about 13 weeks to produce a bloom. A caryopteris pruned at the same time will not flower till towards the end of summer.

FLOWERING ON THE PREVIOUS SEASON'S GROWTH

Examples of shrubs in this group are rhododendron, forsythia, and lilac. Pruning is normally done as soon as the shrub has finished flowering, so that it has the maximum time possible to push out new growth, ripen it, and form the buds that will bear the flowers the following year—usually in spring or early summer.

There is a third, very much smaller group which flowers on spurs on older wood . . .

FLOWERING ON SPURS
(Examples: chaenomeles, wisteria).

Pruning of such shrubs should begin as soon as the flowers fade, shortening the side shoots to about six inches and then, in winter, further pruning to two or three buds. The summer pruning helps the young wood to ripen and encourages the formation of spurs which carry the flowers.

I cannot over-emphasise the importance of keeping a shrub in good health. Regularly remove dead, damaged or diseased growth, and make sure that you have cut back into healthy wood. Avoid any overcrowding in the centre of a bush, but always bear in mind its natural habit. If it becomes necessary to get rid of an old, unproductive shrub, remove the branches, saw through the main stem close to the ground, and dig out the roots. If you leave a stump there is a danger of attack by honey fungus, which may then spread to other subjects. If digging out is impracticable, bore a few holes, not less than half-inch diameter, into the bole or stump, fill them

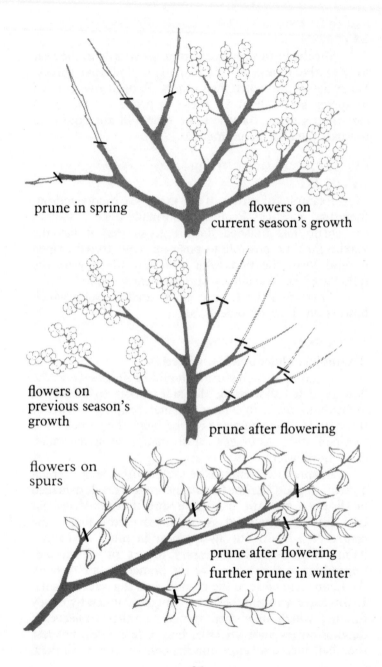

prune in spring

flowers on
current season's growth

flowers on
previous season's
growth

prune after flowering

flowers on
spurs

prune after flowering
further prune in winter

with SBK (a brushwood killer) or sulphuric acid, and seal the holes with clay or putty. Within a few months the wood should have rotted sufficiently for it to be removed or burned.

A word about reversion. Many shrubs have variegated forms, with foliage of more than one colour. You will find many examples in a nursery catalogue: plants with leaves edged or marked with silver or white, yellow or red. These variegated forms are usually weaker than the original type, and after some years you will often find a shoot whose leaves do not bear the variegation. Cut these out as soon as they appear, or the whole shrub will fairly quickly revert to its ordinary plain-leafed habit.

Some gardeners believe that, because shrubs quickly settle into the pattern of a garden and grow with little or no attention, they never need feeding. But even the most fertile soils can be exhausted over a period of years. With shrubs that need little or no pruning, an annual mulch of leaf mould or peat, plus a generous scattering of bone meal, will keep them happy. But shrubs that are pruned hard each year, like hybrid tea or floribunda roses, must be compensated with fairly heavy feedings in the form of manure or other suitable organic fertiliser (Guideline 10). In the same way a shrub that undergoes drastic pruning to rejuvenate it must also receive heavy feeding in its convalescence to help it to steady recovery.

Be quite sure *why* you have your secateurs or pruning saw in your hand before you begin work on a shrub. Take a long look at it, decide exactly what you are aiming at, make the necessary cuts—and then stop! Over-enthusiastic pruning can do much more damage than under-pruning.

CHAPTER FIVE

How to Prune Your Roses

If I had a fiver for every book and article I've read on rose pruning I'd be able to afford a long holiday. And if I'd taken action on all the varied advice I've been offered, I might now be too scared to touch them at all. As always, my rose pruning methods are based on (a) those Ten Guidelines I've urged you to learn, and (b) on years of close observation of how roses behave when pruned in different ways—or not at all. Not at all? Well, if you want to know what happens, go on a country walk in summer and look out for dog roses growing in the hedgerows. Take a close look. See those long, leggy stems with tufty growth at the top bearing the flowers? That's what will happen if you leave a rose unpruned.

"But I do prune my roses every spring," you may say, "and I still get bare-legged rose bushes." The mistake here is that you have overlooked Guideline 5— the one about young wood being more productive. To ensure a succession of young growth, and consequently a bush well furnished from top to bottom, it is necessary to cut back one old stem each year almost to the ground. This will force a new shoot from a basal bud (second part of Guideline 1). Now take a look at one of your hybrid tea bushes, and check where you made your last pruning cut on one of the stems. From that pruned stem, two or three shoots will have resulted, perhaps four if you were very lucky. But how many buds below those shoots remained dormant? Two, three? Then that's two or three too many. You are encouraging leggy growth.

Admittedly, varieties differ in vigour, and soil and climate can affect their behaviour too. But, as a general guide, no year-old stem is going to be persuaded to produce shoots from more than three of its buds, or four at the very most. So there's your problem solved: Aim to prune to the third bud from the base—though sometimes (as you will see in a minute) the second or fourth may be better.

Now please recall two more Guidelines—No. 2, about sap rising strongest to the topmost bud; and No. 7, about keeping the centre of a shrub open as an important health and production measure. I need hardly point out that if you prune down to a bud that is not facing outwards (and this is the most important bud) you will have your main shoot growing either inwards towards the centre, or crossing the path of a neighbouring shoot. So avoid this by always pruning to an outward facing bud— this, you now see, is why it may sometimes be preferable to use the second or fourth bud.

Apart from avoiding unsightliness, pruning to build up a rose with its productive wood arising close to the ground has important practical advantages. It is less top

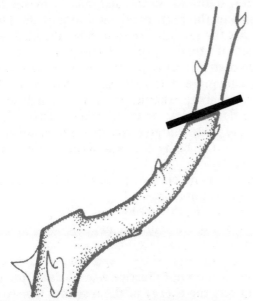

Always prune to an outward-facing bud.

29

heavy, and it is less vulnerable to strong winds which can topple it, loosen its roots, or form a hole around the stem that can lead to water-logging. And it has less distance over which to pass up its food supplies.

When should roses be pruned? The popular idea is late March. There are two drawbacks to pruning as late as this. First, most of us want our roses in bloom as early as possible. And secondly, if it's a warm spring, shoots on the roses can well be 6—8 inches long by the end of March. To prune them off is a waste of the plant's energy, putting an extra strain on its resources: and, with the sap running fast, the cuts easily 'bleed'—a further waste.

Another school of thought asserts that roses can be pruned at any time they are dormant, and that the buds will then break naturally in their own good time, depending on the weather. The main objection is that, in dormancy, there is no sap to heal the cuts. Moisture has time to enter, this can then be frozen, cells can burst, and die-back can follow.

The best solution—simple and safe—is to watch for the first signs of the buds breaking into growth. That's the signal that the sap has begun to flow, the bush is on the move, and it's time to prune. There you have a much better guide than the calendar. In a cold spring you will be starting later; in a mild one, earlier than usual. You need not worry about whether to prune the hybrid teas first, or the floribundas, or the climbers. That tell-tale swelling of the buds will give you the right answer.

Right—you're ready to start. Keep in mind your main objects:-
1. Producing as much growth as possible on as little old wood as possible;
2. Keeping the bush healthy and vigorous, with its centre open to the sun and air;
3. Achieving a shapely, well-balanced plant.

Whatever the type of rose, you must always begin by removing all the unproductive wood—dead, too old, too weak. Divert the energy of the rose into the strong, healthy stems—they are the ones that will give you the best blooms. This applies to all types of rose. Let's take them in turn:-

HYBRID TEAS:

Hybrid teas are the highly successful result of cross-breeding the world's best species and varieties. They produce large, handsome blooms singly or, if allowed, in small clusters. Examples are Peace, Super Star, Wendy Cussons, Fragrant Cloud, Red Devil. The first pruning after planting is a vital one for the proper development of a sound framework. Each strong stem (there should be three, even four, a point to watch when buying) should be pruned down to about three buds— two, perhaps, or four, but always to an outward-facing one. The following spring, the resulting growths are again pruned to about three buds, again outward-facing. Pruning in this way will gradually increase the height of the basic structure—though, of course, each growth bud can produce a summer shoot two, three or more feet

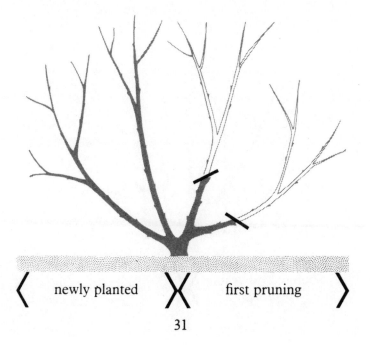

⟨ newly planted ✕ first pruning ⟩

31

long, depending on the vigour of the variety. But the bush will never become tall and ungainly because—remember?—every year from the second pruning onwards at least one of the oldest stems is cut almost to the ground, to the lowest dormant bud you can find. In that way the bush is always furnished with young wood.

Hybrid teas bloom in two main flushes—the first in early to mid-summer, the second in late summer. This second flush blooms mainly on secondary growths, shoots springing from those that have carried the first flush. So a little summer pruning is desirable to ensure a good "second house" performance. Some of this pruning happens automatically when blooms are cut for decoration—when doing this take care always to cut just above an outward-pointing leaf, for in the axil is the bud which will then begin to grow. All stems that are not already cut should be pruned down to an outward leaf about half way down the stem. Spread this work over a few days so that the bush does not suffer shock by losing too much foliage

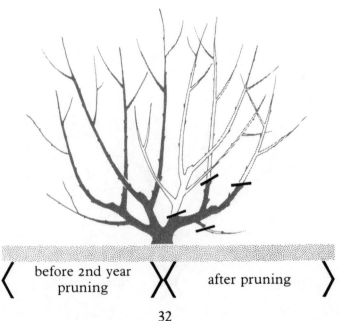

⟨ before 2nd year pruning ⟩ ⟨ after pruning ⟩

at once. In autumn, any overlong stems that might cause the bush to rock in the wind, causing a hole at the base, should be shortened.

Is harder pruning than that described above ever justified? Yes—if you want to exhibit, or you have a particular love of large blooms and are prepared to accept fewer flowers. Then you will prune down to one or two buds instead of three. This will mean fewer shoots, fewer flower buds, all closer to the supply lines and therefore stronger. Hence the larger blooms of—hopefully, anyway—higher quality.

To recap: Cut out all dead, ageing or weak wood. Prune to about three buds, with the top one outward facing. Once the bush is established, cut at least one stem per year to a single bud near ground level. After the first flush, prune the flowered stems by about half, and feed.

FLORIBUNDAS

The flowers of floribundas are produced in clusters, almost continuously from before mid-summer till autumn.

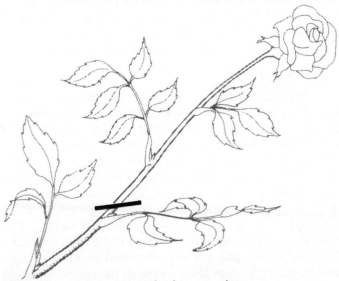

When you cut a rose make it a pruning cut

With some modern varieties the individual flowers resemble those of hybrid teas in form. Floribunda examples: Evelyn Fison, Elizabeth of Glamis, Dearest, Orange Sensation, Allgold.

Pruning of new bushes is exactly the same as for hybrid teas. And if you follow the same method for established bushes you won't go far wrong—always remembering to cut at least one stem right down each year. But there is an improved technique which guarantees a more continuous succession of bloom (rather than flushes) and keeps the bushes always well furnished with young growth. It is this: Start by pruning the newly planted bush to about three buds on each strong stem (remove any weak ones). The resulting shoots will flower later the same year. The following spring prune only lightly, down to the first plump bud on each strong stem. During the ensuing season, two or three strong basal shoots are likely to be thrown up, blooming in later summer. The next spring (third pruning) these one-year-old stems are merely tipped down to the first good bud, but all the two year-old wood is cut hard to a bud near ground level. This may seem drastic, but if you follow it out you will always have a bush with plenty of bloom on wood that is either one or two years old—never more—and a bush that is always compact and never leggy.

STANDARDS

Standards, (H. T. or floribunda) have their heads on a bare stem 3½—4 ft tall. They are popular because they provide height in a rose bed, or make an attractive border to a path, and present their blooms for close appreciation at near nose-level. The heads are a long way from the roots and therefore are not so easily supplied with food as bushes. So slightly harder pruning is desirable to compensate. Start by cutting back to about two buds (the top one, as always, outward-facing). The second year and thereafter prune to two or three buds, but rarely four, and cut one stem back hard to a single bud at the base. Aim always to keep the centre open and the growth young.

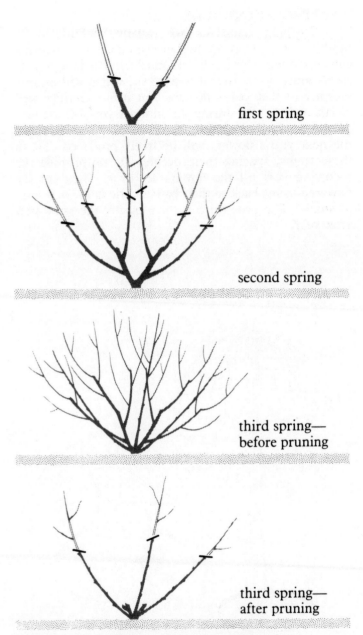

first spring

second spring

third spring—
before pruning

third spring—
after pruning

Floribunda pruning method – drastic but wise

35

WEEPING STANDARDS

Weeping standards are usually wichuriana, or rambler types. They are best grown on a pole to which a galvanised wire "umbrella" is attached. The first year all stems must be shortened to 6—8 in. which will mean a sacrifice of that year's flowers. But it is a sacrifice well worth making, for during the summer you will see new growth gradually lengthening, on which—from laterals—the next year's flowers will be freely produced. Tie in these stems, spacing them evenly. Do no pruning the following year till the flowers are over. Then cut the flowered stems back to their base and tie in the new crop of stems. The procedure is then exactly the same year after year.

Training a weeping standard

RAMBLERS

Ramblers are mainly hybrids of the wichuriana species whose habit of making vigorous new basal growth while the one-year-old stems are producing flowers I have just described. Pruning is, of course, on the same principle—cut out the flowered stems, train in the new—though in some cases you may find there is not enough replacement growth springing from ground level, but some arising from half way up a one-year-old stem. The best of these shoots may be retained but always cut them to the ground when they have flowered. The new growth each year is easily recognised because it is of lighter green and carries no laterals.

CLIMBERS

Broadly there are two kinds of climbers, those that are called 'perpetual' and flower more or less continuously from early summer till autumn, and those—usually

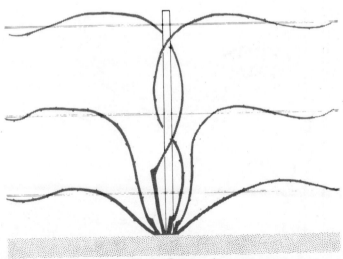

A rambler with last year's flowered stems cut out

"sports" of hybrid tea varieties—that bloom mainly in two flushes. Others may bloom only once a year. By their nature, climbers flower well on older wood for many years, and therefore pruning is much lighter. Newly-planted, they should be cut back moderately in order to give the roots a chance to build up without having to support too much top growth. There is a chance that hybrid tea sports may sometimes resent this, and revert to bush form, but it is a risk worth taking. In succeeding years, merely tip the leading stems and shorten the side shoots to two or three buds. In later years, cut an occasional stem right down to give more room for a younger one. Climbers flower much more freely when trained horizontally or diagonally (Guideline 9)—this slows the upward surge of sap and stimulates the production of the laterals which produce the flowers. When grown up poles or pergolas, twist the stems around in a spiral.

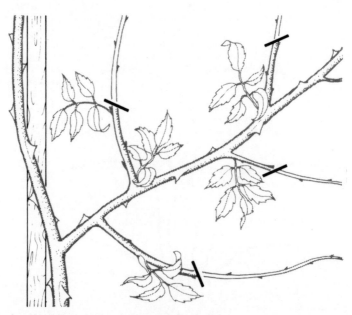

A climbing rose: shorten the laterals

SHRUB ROSES

The term shrub rose embraces the species, the so-called 'old-fashioned' roses, and the many hybrid types that have been evolved from them—one of the biggest and most popular classes is the hybrid musk. Generally they are too large to be thought of as plants for beds, rather as flowering shrubs.

Most shrub roses throw up long stems from the base on which side shoots form. These carry flowers, and then the side shoots break again to bear more flowers and so on. In the end the branch exhausts itself and dies. So the pattern of pruning is this:- Do no pruning the first year after planting. The next year remove any weak growth and shorten the main stems only enough to keep them of even length. After another year or two, it will generally be possible to cut one of the main stems to near ground level to stimulate new basal growth and so keep the wood young over the years. Side shoots may be shortened a little each year, while dormant, if more store is put on the quality of the blooms than the quantity, but I think it best to leave the lovely shrub roses to grow as naturally as possible, while keeping them healthy and well balanced.

OLD LEGGY BUSHES

Roses of all types that have been neglected and have become tall, gaunt and unkempt can often be rejuvenated by cutting the thick woody stems down to within inches of the ground. The work should be spread over at least two years. How do you know at which point to apply your pruning saw (that's the tool you will almost certainly need)? Look closely and you should find, well hidden in the bark, a crescent-shaped scar which signifies a dormant bud. Cut just above it and, if the wound is more than three-quarters of an inch across, paint it with a sealant. To encourage breaks from this old wood, feed the roots—with farmyard, stable, or bagged concentrated manure backed up, later in the year, with rose fertiliser.

SUCKERS

Species roses grow on their own roots and so do roses grown from cuttings or seed. But budded (grafted) roses are likely to throw up long shoots called suckers. These arise from the rootstock on which the variety has been budded. With bush roses the 'union' (juncture of the rootstock and the bud from which the top growth has developed) should be—if planted correctly—just below ground level. With standards, the union is immediately below the head and rootstock growth may emerge on the otherwise bare long stem. Suckers are generally of a lighter green, with smaller leaves than the variety, and—if grown on rugosa stock—will bear a profusion of thin thorns.

It is important to remove suckers as soon as they are seen so that they do not rob the wanted part of the plant of food. If they arise on the stems of standards, simply pull them off. If they spring from the soil, you must

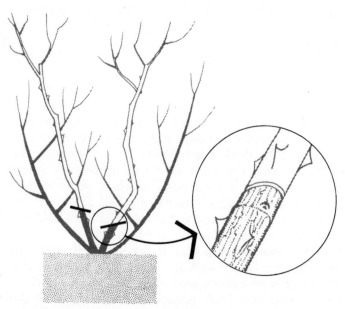

How to rejuvenate and old bush

follow the sucker to its source—usually a strong root. If possible, pull off the sucker, first placing your foot over the root so that you don't pull that up too. If that proves beyond you, cut off the sucker with a knife. Because suckers have 'guard buds' as a defence, a cut sucker will usually replace itself. But as long as you conscientiously remove each one as it appears, your roses will not suffer.

FEEDING

I must. keep on underlining the fact that the removal of top growth by pruning should always go hand in hand with the feeding of the roots (Guideline 10). With roses, well rotted farmyard manure is hard to beat if applied as a mulch after pruning (in cold districts, wait till the soil has warmed up a little). If you cannot get farmyard manure, use peat or specially prepared bark as your mulch. Mulches need to be backed up with a well-balanced fertiliser containing not only the 'Big Three'—nitrogen (for leaf and stem growth), phosphates (for root development and earlier flowering) and potash (for health and flower quality)—but also important trace elements such as magnesium, iron, and calcium. These 'extras' are found in the reliable proprietary rose fertilisers. An application—always at the recommended rate and no more—immediately after pruning and another after the first flush of bloom is normally sufficient. In the second case, pull any mulch away from the bush, sprinkle the fertiliser, and water it in before replacing the mulch.

CHAPTER SIX

Climbers, Wall Shrubs and Hedges

The imaginative use of climbers and wall shrubs can transform a dull-looking house into an entrancing one, an unsightly wall or fence into a thing of beauty. As always, the choice of subjects must be made with care, and nothing should be planted without full knowledge of its habit, ultimate size, and colour. Aspect is important, too: almost any subject will flourish on the sunny side of a house; only a few—though they include such attractive ones as camellia, hydrangea petiolaris, and pyracantha— do well on the north or east side. It is sometimes possible to give a climber full rein, and let it ramble at will over an outhouse or through the branches of an old tree. The Russian Vine (polygonum baldschuanicum), clematis montana, and wisteria are particularly happy in this role. Not so vigorous, but also willing to roam, are some vigorous species of rose, clematis flammula, and most of the honeysuckles. All these can be left unpruned except for a bit of tidying up here and there. But in most gardens today, climbers and wall shrubs need regular pruning not only to control them, but to help them give the best possible performance.

While a few climbers are capable of gripping a smooth surface such as a wall—Virginia creeper and ivies are examples—most need support of some kind to which they can attach tendrils or twining growths, or to which their long stems can be tied. Against a wall, strong wires fixed horizontally to wall nails or, better still, eye bolts with strainers to keep the wires taut, are as convenient a support as any. The wires should be spaced in tiers 9—18 inches apart, depending on the nature of the climber. Large-mesh plastic coated trellis has now replaced the

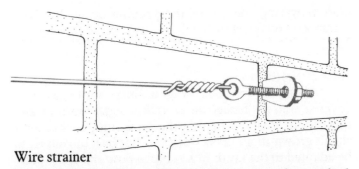

Wire strainer

less durable wooden trellis that was commonly attached to walls, and this is excellent for the smaller climbers, such as clematis hybrids, and the less vigorous roses. Pergolas make superb hosts for climbing roses, wisteria, clematis, and honeysuckle. Single poles and arches can also be attractively decorated.

It is important when planting a shrub or climber against a wall or fence to leave a space of at least 9 inches, and preferably 12, between plant and wall. In that way the roots can get a reasonable supply of rain, so important to the early development of the subject. Newly-planted climbers should normally be pruned back by a half to two thirds. In some cases strong growth will quickly spring from the base of the plant and the original stems can then be cut to ground level. In the second year a start can be made to training the climber. Initially the young stems should be led out in a fan, leaving good space between each. Unwanted or weak growths can be removed altogether. The leaders should be shortened each winter in the early years to keep them growing strongly, and side shoots not wanted for filling a space can be pruned back by about half. Evergreen climbers should be pruned more lightly than deciduous ones. As the climber gets well established, as many of the main stems as possible should be pulled down to grow horizontally or at a low angle. This causes a modest check in the sap flow but increases the production of flowers. The timing of pruning closely follows the rules for pruning shrubs: those that flower on the current season's growth are pruned in winter or early spring, and those on the previous year's growth as soon as possible after flowering (details of the pruning of all the more common climbing shrubs will be found in the Alphabetical List).

WALL SHRUBS

A wall shrub is simply an ordinary shrub grown to cover a wall or fence, or to give it extra warmth and protection. Pruning follows the same lines as that for a shrub grown in an open situation, but has, of course, to be adapted to the needs of its special position. If the plant you have chosen has a single stem, it must be headed back in early spring to ensure the early development of side shoots which, by annual tipping back, will form the framework of the shrub. Always remember, when seeking to balance a shrub, that hard pruning produces stronger reaction than light (Guideline 3), and that weak shoots should be cut harder than vigorous ones. If a bud pointing in the desired direction fails to break, it can usually be induced to do so by notching—cutting the bark just above the bud—before the sap begins to rise. (Notching—See p. 18).

For obvious reasons, the growth of a wall shrub must be confined, to keep it tidily against the wall. Laterals that start growing outwards are cut back, but wholesale clipping or pruning must be timed to match the habit of the shrub. One flowering on the current season's growth can be cut back hard in early spring, one flowering on older wood not until the flowers have faded. In either case, only enough young growth should be left to fill any available spaces; and from time to time the shrub may benefit by the complete removal of some of the oldest wood to make room for new.

HEDGES

A hedge is a series of shrubs—usually, but not always, of the same kind—grown to form a barrier or separating feature, and trained and maintained by regular pruning. It may be thick and impenetrable, shaped and trimmed as immaculately as a French poodle, or loose-growing and graceful. Early training depends on the habit of the shrub chosen, and details will be found in the Alphabetical List. Grown as a garden boundary, a close-growing hedge of neat appearance is the normal requirement. The aim must always be to develop and keep it with the top markedly narrower than the base. There are two main reasons for this: first, such a shape enables more light to reach the lower branches and shoots of the hedge, thereby keeping the base well furnished and, second, to prevent its keeling over from the weight of snow, which can be considerable.

The larger leafed hedge shrubs, such as laurel, should be pruned with secateurs, but those with smaller leaves—privet, thorn, yew—are best trimmed with shears or an electric trimmer. Unless you are very experienced and have a good eye, a line stretched between two stakes at the required height will ensure that you cut the hedge to the correct level and height. All trimmings should be cleared from the hedge and the best way to collect them is to spread a sheet (cloth or plastic) alongside: that avoids much sweeping up. Most hedges can be safely trimmed at any time between late spring and late summer—even three or four times in that period if you are very keen about neatness. If you cut later than late summer, young shoots can be damaged by frost. Don't forget that every time you trim your hedge you are taking a crop off it, and that you should compensate the soil with a feed of manure or other organic fertiliser once or twice a year. You will be amply rewarded by the glowing health and vigour of your hedge!

TOPIARY

The art of training and clipping trees and shrubs into special shapes, especially of animals or birds, is called topiary. It is less popular than it was in the days of more formal gardening, but still has its fascination. Yew, box, holly and privet can all be used, and the shaping is done with secateurs and shears, usually in summer. A strong metal or wire frame is necessary for the more intricate shapes, the developing shoots being tied on to it at frequent intervals.

CHAPTER SEVEN

Fruit – Simple Ways to Success

Every true gardener cherishes a desire to grow beautiful, luscious fruit—apples with clear shining skins, sun-warmed pears, peaches with that lovely velvety bloom on their cheeks, bunches of ripe grapes. The list is as long as it is enticing.

The gardener can choose and plant his trees with care, on a good site and in the right soil. But he won't get the top quality fruit he is looking forward to without proper pruning. Left to themselves, the trees and bushes will become thickets of branches and shoots, bearing well at first, but then producing smaller and smaller fruit as the years go by until disease or exhaustion brings their life to a premature end.

The three over-riding reasons for pruning fruit trees are SHAPE, HEALTH, and QUALITY. You may ask "Why not include *size* of tree? I've only a modest garden and my fruit trees have to be kept small." Well, small trees are certainly not only necessary when space is limited but also highly desirable—whatever the size of the garden. For they make cultivation so much easier. You can reach to prune them, spray the top branches as well as the lower ones, and pick the fruit without endangering life and limb perched atop a ladder.

So, if you are about to start growing apples or pears, plums or peaches, don't think in terms of limiting their size by pruning—think of *rootstocks*. The way to make sure that the tree, throughout its life, will be comfortably manageable is to insist that your nurseryman supplies one grafted on to a dwarfing, or semi-dwarfing rootstock. The rootstock governs the size of the tree, and you should choose one that is right for your garden and soil.

For apples—the fruit I am going to deal with first—the dwarfest rootstock of all is M9, which rarely produces trees more than 7—8 ft tall. They are planted 8—10 ft apart. Such trees come into bearing very quickly but are not suitable for thin soil or poor growing conditions, and always need a stake. The ideal rootstock for most modern gardens, in my view, is M26. The trees will eventually reach a height of around 10—12 ft, but even when fully mature you will never need more than a short ladder or pair of steps to collect the fruit. Planting distance is 12—15 ft. Alternatives are MM106 or M7: on poor or shallow soils MM106 can replace M9 if you want a really dwarf tree.

SHAPE

Shape is determined by the early pruning of the tree. There are several classic shapes, but the modern gardener, I believe, is not so much concerned with appearance as the amount and quality of the fruit he can get for the minimum outlay.

Some experts are always urging us to grow fruit as *cordons*, which means on a single stem. "What an excellent boundary a row of cordons makes," they say. "How well they look, how easy to maintain!" All this is true, but you are rarely told that a nursery will charge you as much for a cordon as a young tree, or that the quantity of apples you can expect from a cordon in full bearing averages about 5 lb, whereas a bush tree on a semi-dwarfing rootstock will commonly yield many times as much.

Espaliers (trees grown with horizontally opposing branches, usually against a wall or fence) yield barely half the amount of fruit compared with a bush tree, and cost almost twice as much to buy—although, as you will see, you can save money (but not time) by training your own espalier from a maiden (one-year-old tree).

Cordons and espaliers can, of course, have a useful place in the garden, and I shall not ignore them, but when it comes to the nitty-gritty of economics (which few can afford to overlook these days) my advice is to go for

47

apples or pears, plums or peaches grown as bushes on semi-dwarfing rootstocks.

HEALTH

Everyone knows that children—and adults—grow frail and sickly if deprived of light, fresh air, and food. So do plants if they get less than their fair share, and overcrowding of branches, particularly in the centre of a tree, must be avoided. Keeping the middle open admits the sunlight to help ripening and pollination, and ensures that sprays against pest and disease reach all parts.

Damaged or diseased wood must generally be removed whenever seen, cutting right back to healthy growth. Some varieties—as well as uncared for trees—are likely to develop canker and since it may well spread to kill the branch, and eventually the tree, it must be treated at the earliest opportunity if surgery is to be avoided. First scrub the affected area with a wire brush to get it as clean as possible, then paint it over with Medo or Arbrex.

QUALITY

Fruit that is unblemished, of good size, and well-flavoured is largely the result of correct pruning and adequate feeding, for the well-being of the tree or bush depends on the correlation of the two.

Once you have planted a fruit tree, it is important to learn and always keep in mind three key objectives:-

1. To build up a well-balanced framework by means of early hard pruning.
2. To bring the tree gradually into full bearing with lighter pruning. And finally
3. To maintain a balance between the continued production of healthy new growth and of good quality fruit.

These objectives apply to all kinds of fruit.

APPLES

The cheapest and simplest tree you can buy is called a maiden—with one year's growth after it

48

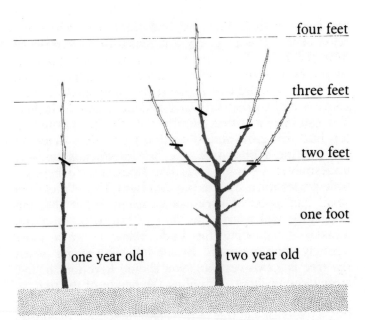

four feet

three feet

two feet

one foot

one year old   two year old

Starting an apple or pear

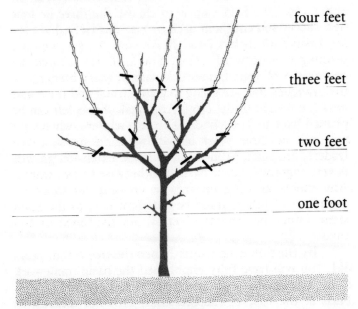

four feet

three feet

two feet

one foot

The framework after three years

49

has been grafted. You will find the union, where the scion of the chosen variety was joined to the rootstock, near the base of the stem. Don't bury this union: it should be 3—4 inches above soil level. Your first pruning act, as soon as the tree is planted, is simple: cut to just above a bud so that you have a stem of 24—27 inches. You can leave it at that, but if you do the shoot from that top bud will grow almost vertically and this—since we are creating a bush tree, the best production unit—is undesirable: we want spreading branches. So here's a little professional trick to put that right. Cut a "nick"—a small half-moon of bark—immediately below that top bud. This will restrict the flow of sap to the bud and weaken it, allowing the buds below to grow more strongly—and outwards. By the following winter (when the tree is a two-year-old) you should have four or five strong young shoots, doubling the height of the tree.

If you like to spend a little more money, you can buy a two-year-old tree in this condition—and, of course, you reduce your waiting period for fruit by one year. In either case, the next step is to choose the three or four best shoots and cut them back by two-thirds, so that they are around 10 inches long. Make sure the bud you are pruning to is outward facing. You have now created the beginnings of your framework with primary branches— the branches that are going to grow strong and thick and bear the weight of the crop. Any weak shoots left can be pruned back to 3 or 4 buds. The next winter—when your tree will be three years old—those main stems, called leaders, are again pruned back. If the extension growth is very vigorous, cut it by half: otherwise to two-thirds. Any shoots growing inwards or crossing (or threatening to cross) others must be cut right out, to the main stem. Other side-shoots (laterals) are shortened to 4–5 buds.

By the following winter, when the tree is four years old, you will have fully established the basic framework of the tree, and you should have quite a number of fruit buds at the base of the branches. It is not difficult to recognise these: they are plump, scaly, and—in the case

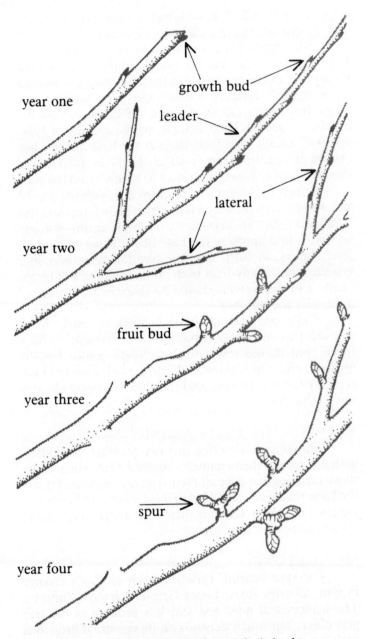

year one

growth bud

leader

year two

lateral

fruit bud

year three

spur

year four

Branches showing growth buds and fruit buds

51

of pears—pointed. A growth bud, by contrast, is smaller and lies flat against the shoot.

Fruit buds normally form on two-year-old wood. Let's get this quite clear because it is important. Suppose you prune a stem in the late autumn of 1984, the top bud (at least) will produce a shoot the next summer, and when the leaves fall in autumn (1985) it will have a number of growth buds along it. By the autumn of 1986, you will usually find fruit buds at the base of the shoot (unless it is a tip bearer—which I will be referring to shortly—in which case there may be a fruit bud at the end).

A fruit bud normally develops a very short, stubby and woody stem on which more fruit buds form, and this is called a spur. So—taking our example again—you can expect to find spurs at the base of the shoot in autumn 1987. Spurs, in turn, develop over the years into spur systems, with many fruit buds. In time, there will be too many, and the systems should be shortened and thinned to restrict the number.

While establishing the framework or, later, when you want to encourage a bud to break strongly to fill a space, you should resort to "notching", which has the opposite effect to nicking. This time a half-moon of bark is cut just above the bud, and this diverts a larger share of sap to that bud.

HELPING THE FRUIT ALONG

I am going to describe just two pruning methods—without giving them names:- *Method One* which suits those varieties that bear all their fruit on spurs (and that's the large majority), and *Method Two* for the tip bearers—varieties that bear some of their fruit at the ends of the shoots. Here they are in detail:-

METHOD ONE

For spur-bearing varieties (such as Cox's Orange Pippin, Charles Ross, James Grieve, Laxton's Superb). The leaders will need less and less pruning as the tree gets older, but much depends on its vigour. If growth is very strong, merely tip the leaders, always to a bud; if weak, prune the previous year's growth back by a quarter to a third. This will cause buds farther down to break and form laterals. If you leave the laterals unpruned, they will certainly form fruit buds in their second year, but the tree will become overcrowded, the lower branches will be weighed down to the ground, and buds towards the base of each shoot will remain dormant, leaving a length of bare (and unproductive) stem. So, as a general rule, prune laterals back to 4, 5, or even 6 buds: if you prune harder—say to 3 or 4 buds—the effect will be to stimulate growth buds at the expense of fruit buds. Secondary growth (sub-laterals) forming on the pruned lateral should be shortened back to one bud unless required to fill a space. When fruit spurs have formed, the laterals may be cut right back to them if sufficient growth is being made elsewhere. This procedure is carried out in exactly the same way from year to year, but each time the needs of the tree must be assessed afresh. Is it making too much growth at the expense of fruit buds? Then you must prune more lightly, merely tipping the leaders, leaving some of the laterals unpruned. Are too many fruit spurs forming, with a lack of new growth shoots? Then prune harder—the extension of growth of the leaders by a quarter to a third, the laterals to 2 or 3 buds. In this way you can maintain a correct balance.

METHOD TWO

For tip-bearing varieties such as Worcester Pearmain, Beauty of Bath, Bramley Seedling, Tydeman's Early. The leaders are treated in the same way as in Method One. But, because fruit buds form on the ends of many of the laterals, it would be wrong to prune them all. It would be equally wrong to leave them all, for the reasons already explained in Method One. So the sensible solution is to leave a third to a half of the longer laterals unpruned, and to shorten those less than 8 inches long and not showing terminal fruit buds to about 5 buds. This will induce the production of fresh laterals while allowing some fruit buds to form at their base (it is rare for all the crop to be formed at the tips). As in Method

53

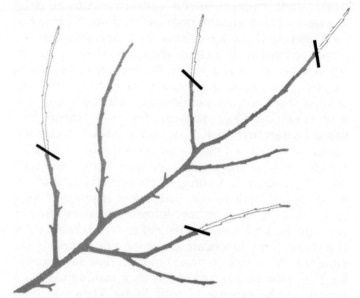

How to prune a tip-bearer

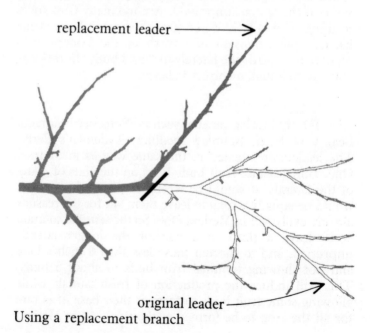

replacement leader ———→

original leader ———
Using a replacement branch

54

One, some laterals that have fruited can be spurred right back.

And there you have it! One simple method for each of the two types of tree. There are just two points to make clear. Till now, I have generally advised you to prune to outward-pointing buds, for two main reasons: (1) so that the shoots grow away from the centre of the tree, leaving it open (Guideline 7); and (2) so that branches will develop a horizontal, or wide-angled habit, on which fruit buds develop much more readily (Guideline 9). But as the tree matures you may well find that a branch or shoot is bending so low that you want the shoots from it to grow in a more vertical direction. So it is then wise to prune to the bud that is pointing upward rather than outward. Put in another way, always prune to a bud facing in the desired direction. With an open-centred bush tree, lower branches are sometimes borne down to the ground by the weight of fruit. Two or three years before actual touchdown, earmark a suitable lateral on the upper side of the branch and a few feet back from its tip. Shorten it a little each year to keep it growing vigorously so that, when the time comes, you can cut the old branch back to it, using your prepared stem as a replacement.

It is worth knowing that fruit buds form more readily on the weaker shoots: on strong ones only if they are well-angled from the vertical.

CORDONS

Cordons are usually grafted on semi-dwarfing stocks and grown on a single straight stem. Double and triple cordons have single stems arising, low down, from the same trunk. It is normal for maidens to be planted—scion uppermost, 2½–3 ft apart—at an angle of 45 deg. and tied to a long bamboo cane which is in turn attached to taut horizontal wires spaced about 2 feet apart. If possible, the row should run north and south. No pruning need be done after planting. The next winter all side shoots should be shortened to 4 buds. The leader is normally left to grow on unpruned until it reaches as far as you want it: then it can be tipped each spring. Annual pruning of a cordon is straightforward—and is always done in the second half of summer, as the laterals begin to ripen and get a little woody at the base. They won't all ripen at once, so spread the work as necessary.

Those growing directly from the main stem are pruned to three leaves (not counting the basal cluster), those arising from existing laterals (pruned the previous summer) or from spurs to one leaf. Any secondary growth from a pruned shoot occurring later in the summer is cut back to one bud from its point of origin. A few of the longer laterals may be pruned back to fruit buds each year: how many depends on how much new growth is available. As the cordon lengthens over the years, spur systems usually need thinning. Remove any overcrowding ones altogether, and reduce the number of spurs on others. A little extra length, and therefore more fruit, can be had in later years by untying the cordon and lowering

How to prune a cordon apple

its angle by 5 deg. or so. To avoid secondary growth, don't start summer pruning too soon. In a wet season, it may be better to delay pruning till the dormant season.

ESPALIERS

Espaliers are trees with single vertical trunks and opposing side branches trained horizontally on wires 12–15 inches apart. A semi-dwarfing rootstock is generally employed to produce a medium-sized tree, but dwarfing or vigorous stocks can be used to produce either small or large trees. Medium-sized espaliers should be planted 12–15 ft apart, small 10–12 ft, and large 15–18 ft. Although nurserymen will supply espaliers with two or three tiers already established, it is not difficult—besides being very rewarding and less expensive—to train your own tree from a maiden. After planting against a strong bamboo stake, cut it back to a strong bud a couple of inches above the lowest wire. Allow only the top bud and two below to grow on (make sure these lower buds are opposite and facing along the wire on each side). Rub out all other buds once growth begins from these two. The next winter again cut back the central stem 2 in. above the

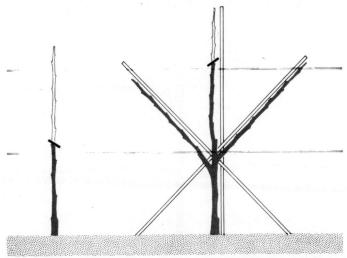

Espalier training – first stages

57

next wire up, and choose another two opposing buds. Repeat the process each year until you have as many tiers as you need. Then cut the central stem back close to the top pair of branches.

That's not quite all. The shoots you leave to grow outwards will grow more vigorously if you tie them in at an angle of about 45 degrees in their first season of growth. If both have made equal growth, you can then tie them down to a horizontal wire the following year. But if one is weaker than the other, lower it only partially for the time being, to allow it to receive more sap than its partner and so catch up in vigour. Each branch is, in effect, a cordon, producing its fruit along a single straight stem. Therefore, pruning is exactly the same as for a cordon from the second summer on. Any shoots arising from the main stem are pinched out, though you may leave the occasional weak one to form fruit buds, and then prune it back to those buds.

Espalier training nearly complete

58

HOW TO PRUNE A NEGLECTED TREE

Fruit trees of some age whose pruning has been neglected, incorrect, or insufficient are all too common. If you move into a new house and are confronted with such a tree in the garden, what can you do? I have never been in favour of keeping incurable patients in my garden, and if the tree is aged and full of canker, it is better to grub it out and plant a new one, which will become increasingly productive. But if the tree seems healthy, tackle it in this way. First, cut out all dead and diseased wood. Next open up the centre of the tree. This will usually mean cutting out one or two major branches. If the tree is vigorous with a mass of unproductive shoots, thin all too-close, crossing, or rubbing branches, and also water shoots (these may form around the edge of a wound caused by the amputation of a branch: rub them off as they appear). Occasionally a strong water shoot may be found growing towards a space that could conveniently be filled. Pruned annually, in the same way

How to prune a neglected tree

59

as a leader on a young tree, such a shoot can become productive.

Tall, or over-long, branches that need not be cut out altogether may be shortened back to a suitable replacement branch, but this should not be less than half the diameter of the parent branch. Spur systems, especially on varieties which form spurs easily, are often far too numerous and large on a tree that has lacked pruning. These should be rigorously thinned, leaving one system every 5–6 inches, and those remaining should be reduced in size to leave no more than a few fruit buds on each. Renovating a neglected tree involves heavy surgery and can inflict a severe shock if done all at once. So, unless the tree is weak and stunted, spread the work over two or three years.

If pruning has been neglected, it's a fair bet that feeding has, too. It becomes all the more important to make good the deficiency as soon as a proportion of the top growth has been removed. Start by clearing a circle 4–6 feet in diameter, depending on the size of the tree, around the trunk. Then apply a generous mulch of farmyard manure or a concentrated manure mixed with leafmould, straw, or peat. If new growth is vigorous, allow grass to grow up to the trunk again (this will absorb surplus nitrogen); if weak, keep the area clear of grass and weeds and feed annually. Ageing and neglected trees inevitably collect moss and lichen on trunks and branches. This can be removed, leaving the bark clean and shining, by spraying thoroughly with Mortegg in mid-winter (you will also be killing off the eggs of aphids and other pests). But spray only every third year.

PEARS

Although pears have slightly different characteristics from apples—principally, that they produce fruit buds more freely and tend not to make quite such strong growth—I am not going to confuse you by suggesting any variation in pruning. Prune pears on exactly the same lines as you prune apples! Just keep the same aims in mind: good health, no overcrowding, plenty of light and air, a sound balance between growth buds and fruit buds. The best rootstocks: Quince A, or C for strong soil.

PLUMS

For the same reasons as with apples and pears, plums are best grown as bushes. The root stock St Julien A produces a bush that can be comfortably handled. Do not expect fruit for five or six years. If you prefer to buy a maiden rather than a two-year-old tree, cut it back in spring to about 3 ft (but to 4½ ft if you prefer a half-standard). Shorten the "feathers" (side shoots) to 2 or 3 inches (these should be left for about three years, shortened annually to five leaves in summer). The next winter choose four good, evenly spaced shoots at the top of the stem and cut them back by half. Prefer wide angled shoots to near-vertical ones. The following year, cut the new growth these leaders have made by a half, and cut out overcrowding, crossing, or rubbing shoots. From

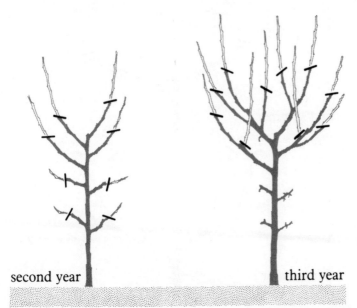

second year   third year

Developing a young plum

61

then on, this is the only kind of pruning that is normally necessary. Always carry it out in July to minimise the danger of infection by silver leaf disease.

FAN TRAINING

Plums—peaches and nectarines too—love a warm wall and the fruit is all the better for it. If you have such a space available, it is well worth growing your plum tree in a fan shape. Fans, like espaliers, can be bought with the early training done, and this saves time. But you can start with a maiden, pruning it down to a couple of feet the first year, and cutting all laterals close to the main stem. In early summer, choose two strong shoots on each side, about 9–12 inches from the ground and tie them first to bamboo canes and then, at about 30 degrees, to horizontal wire supports as they lengthen. All other buds are rubbed out except those at the top of the central stem. The next summer this stem is cut out, and the following February each of the two side branches is pruned to a

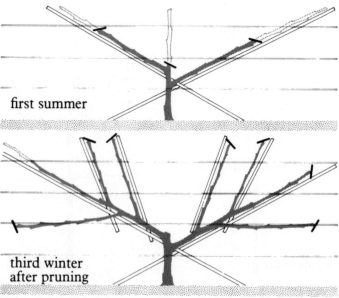

first summer

third winter
after pruning

How to form a fan

bud about 15 inches from the trunk. During the ensuing summer the shoot from the end bud of each, two well spaced shoots on the upper side, and one on the under side should be tied to canes and attached to the tiers of the wire support. Other shoots should be rubbed out. In the following February all branches are pruned back to an upward facing bud, leaving them about 30 inches long.

You now have the main spokes of the framework of your fan established. The leading stems are then trained on, to extend the framework, and some lateral shoots are used to fill spaces or later used as replacements for older shoots. Those growing outwards from the main structure are removed. The tips of all other laterals are pinched out when they have made six leaves. After fruiting, previously shortened shoots are further reduced by half, and any other necessary pruning (mainly removal of unwanted wood) is done. Tie in shoots where necessary, especially any growing vertically.

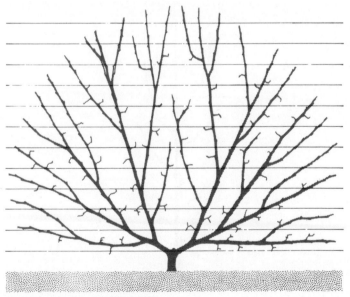

A mature fan-trained tree

PEACHES

Peaches—and nectarines, a form of peach—do best against a south-facing wall, but can be grown very successfully in an open site, providing it is reasonably sheltered. Good drainage is all-important. If you buy a maiden, it will usually have a number of side shoots. As soon as these have made leaves, in late spring, cut back the main stem to 2 or 3 feet, select three or four good side shoots near the top to form the primary branches, and remove the lowest "feathers". But leave others to grow on: these will eventually bear fruit, and when they get weighed down to near the ground they can then be removed. After the initial pruning of the maiden, little pruning is normally necessary beyond the removal of overcrowding or crossing branches, and unwanted basal growth. Should tips of branches die back, prune them down to healthy wood.

The formative pruning of a fan-trained peach is just the same as that for a plum (already described) up to the

A growing peach: early pruning

64

point when, in the third spring, the eight branches of the fan have been cut back to about 30 inches. Let the terminal bud on each grow on as extensions, and remove buds that are growing outwards or in towards the wall. Laterals should now be allowed to grow both above and beneath the branch, at 6 inch intervals (rub out all other buds). When these side shoots are 18–20 inches long, pinch out the ends and tie them in to your wire framework. These shoots will bear blossom and fruit the following year.

From the fourth spring on, annual pruning follows a pattern of thinning shoots, pinching back, tying in . . . and ensuring that there is always a replacement for the shoot that has fruited. You must recognise three types of bud: growth buds, which are slender; fruit buds, which are plump; and triple buds, which have one growth bud and two fruit buds. If all buds on a wall-trained tree were allowed to grow on, the growth buds would smother and weaken the fruit buds, and the crop would be poor. So

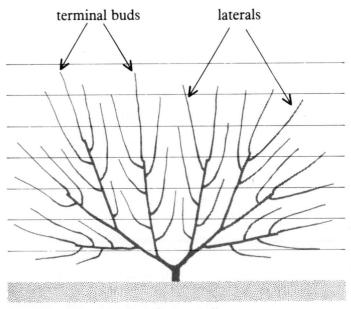

A peach well trained against a wall

thinning, or disbudding, is essential. Examine each young shoot that formed the previous year and you should find both growth and fruit buds along it. Leave one growth bud or, perhaps, two, near the base to grow on as replacement for its parent which, after fruiting, is cut back to that point. Let the terminal bud grow on for the time being, but pinch it back to four leaves when it has made half a dozen leaves or so.

What about the rest of the buds? First, don't touch any of the blossoms. If too many set fruit there is plenty of time to thin the swelling fruits when they reach a half to an inch across (the final thinning should leave a fruit every 6–8 inches). Shoots with leaves—whether with or without blossom—should be spaced every 5 or 6 inches along the parent stem, removing the surplus ones. Those growing out with blossom should be pinched back to two good leaves, others when the growing point is an inch long. You won't find the buds in the right state of development all at the same time, so the work must be

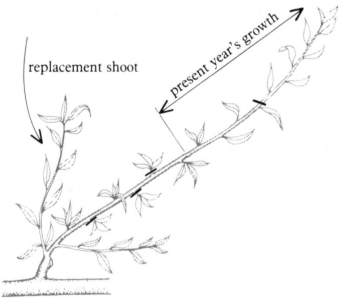

Disbud but leave one (or two) replacement shoots

66

spread over a couple of weeks. When the crop is gathered, the fruited shoots should be cut back to their replacements, except any that may be needed to grow on to fill a space. Remove any dead, damaged or diseased wood at the same time.

A warning: Never prune peaches or other stone fruit in winter!

CHERRIES

Sweet cherries are simply not worth growing in the normal garden. The trees quickly grow tall and it is impossible to protect the fruit from the birds, who will have the lot—or almost. They are not suitable for growing on a wall, which would enable you to net them, so you can't solve the problem that way. In any case sweet cherries need a pollinator, and so at least two trees are necessary. Acid cherries—the Morello is the most popular—are easier. You need only one, since they are self-fertile (able to set their own pollen) and can be grown

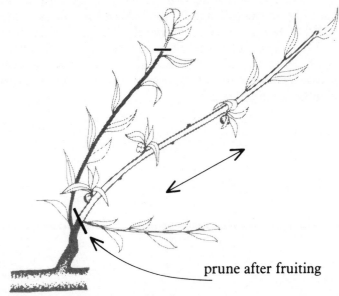

prune after fruiting

Cut back the fruited stem

either as bush trees or against a wall. Other advantages are that they are not too vigorous, don't mind a north wall, and the fruit rarely attracts birds.

Bush trees are treated in much the same way as plums. When well established, cut a few branches back each year to 3-year-old wood, keeping the centre of the tree open. Don't touch the year-old shoots for these bear the fruit. Do all pruning as the buds break in spring. Fan-trained trees can be built up and trained much like peaches, except that shoots need be only 2–3 inches apart.

FIGS

Figs need sun and warmth and—like peaches—yield best against a warm wall. The roots should be contained in some way to an area of about 4 ft by 2 ft, and 3 ft in depth. Once planted, the new growth is trained in a rough fan shape and from the second year, young shoots are pinched out at about the fourth or fifth leaf in midsummer to promote the side shoots which will bear fruit the following year. In early spring, any weak, crossing or frost-damaged wood should be cut out, and healthy shoots showing embryo figs tied in, giving them plenty of space to ripen in late summer. If the roots have not been restricted, it will probably be necessary to root prune from time to time to prevent excessive growth and maintain a good crop.

CHAPTER EIGHT

Soft Fruit Secrets

If pruning soft fruit is easier than top fruit it's only because you are dealing with smaller, more manageable plants. The principles are just as straightforward, varying according to the habit of the subject. If you understand how the berries are formed and how they are borne, everything will fall into place. For easy reference, instructional details are set out in alphabetical order:-

BLACKBERRIES
Including all the hybrids such as the boysenberry, loganberry, and wineberry. Left to grow at will, all these would become rampant and soon get out of hand in the garden. Fortunately they are easy to control if grown along wire supports—which is best—or trained against walls or timber fences, or over arches. New plants should be cut down to 9 inches, and the first season's shoots (which will not fruit till the following year) are tied in fan-wise and evenly spaced out. Do not take them up higher than you can comfortably reach to simplify picking. As soon as the canes have fruited, these are cut to the ground and the new growth that will have been springing up from the base during the summer is tied in, as above, to replace the old. A refinement of training, which makes it easier to sort out the new canes from the old, is to tie in the young growth vertically until the old is cut down. Then it can be trained out ready for the next season's fruiting. Don't worry if, particularly after planting late or if dry weather ensues, growth is slow the first year: it will quickly catch up the second. And remember, when training the canes out, that the more you can get lying

horizontally—though with proper spacing—the bigger will be your crop.

BLUEBERRIES
Plant the bushes 6 ft apart. No pruning is necessary till cropping begins, probably in the third year. Thereafter remove a proportion of the oldest wood each winter. But don't touch strong young shoots: these will carry the best fruit the following year. Blueberries need acid soil, and do well in "rhododendron country".

BLACKCURRANTS
New plants (spaced 6 ft apart and set deeply in the soil) must be cut down drastically, to within an inch of soil level. Thus will cause strong shoots to emerge the following spring and summer, and allow the bushes to

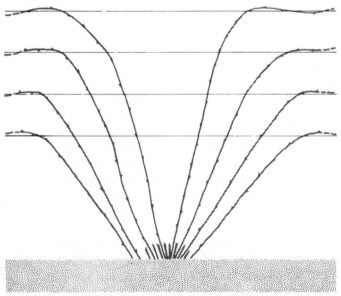

Training blackberries and loganberries

70

establish themselves before being asked to fruit. The next autumn merely tip the strong growths, but cut weak ones to the ground. Prune in this way for the next two or three years. Thereafter prune—as soon after fruiting as is practicable—like this: Cut a quarter to a third of the branches to the ground, starting with the oldest and any that are touching, or near, the ground. Prune others back to young replacement wood. Aim always at trying to leave plenty of strong young growth. As the bushes age, fewer branches should be cut to ground level. Don't bother to look for buds to cut to when pruning black-currants: there are always plenty of tiny ones.

Old bushes—provided they are healthy and not afflicted with big bud disease—can be given a fresh lease of life by cutting them to within a few inches of the ground in autumn. But help them along with heavy manuring and feeding—treatment blackcurrants enjoy at any stage of their lives.

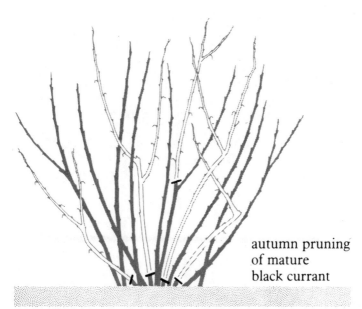

autumn pruning
of mature
black currant

Blackcurrant: encourage the young growth

GOOSEBERRIES

Plant young bushes (usually supplied as two-year-olds) 5 feet apart—but only one foot if cordons are grown—and not too deeply. In the formative years, the aim should be to establish a bush with 8–10 strong branches on a "leg" (bare stem) 6–8 inches above ground level. After planting cut the stems back by half to a good bud. This will be outward-facing if the branches are fairly upright, but upward-facing if drooping (remember this point in subsequent pruning). Thereafter the extension growth made by the leaders is pruned back by about half each year (less if growth is very vigorous, more if it is weak). Laterals are cut to about 6 inches, but down to 2 or 3 if you value size more than quantity. Weak shoots should be removed or pruned right back. As the bushes age, cut out an old branch occasionally, aiming always to keep the centre of the bush well open, and branches off the ground. Unless you can net the bushes

two year old plant
after pruning
in February

Pruning a young gooseberry

72

against birds, which attack the buds, pruning is best deferred to early spring.

GRAPES

Although some successful efforts have been made to grow good crops from outdoor plantings in Britain, these are necessarily confined to the warmer and sunnier districts. But anyone with a glasshouse of sufficient size can secure an excellent crop if the vine is given the right treatment. I am concerned only with the training and pruning.

The simplest and, for the amateur, the best method of training is to set a number of vines 4 ft apart along the side of the greenhouse. Growth is kept to a single stem which is allowed to grow till it reaches the apex. Parallel wires must be stretched across the roof of the house, 9 inches below the glass, to which the growths can be tied in.

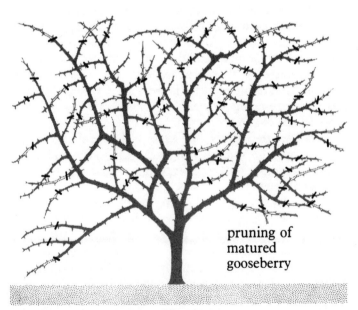

pruning of
matured
gooseberry

An older bush: keep the 'leg' clear

73

So that you don't have to wait several years for a crop, buy a "fruiting vine" in a pot for delivery in late autumn. Keep it in its pot through the winter, and plant it in early spring. Prune it back to a strong bud about a month before you plant.

Allow one strong shoot at the top to grow up, pinching out any side shoots at two leaves. Stop the growing point of the leading shoot when it is about 6 ft tall. Choose a strong resulting shoot near the tip and train it up as the leader. The other side shoots can be allowed to grow till mid-September, when they should be stopped.

When all leaves have fallen, again prune back the leading stem to about 5 ft, and the laterals to two buds. The following year, the leader should reach the apex of the house. At that point pinch it out. Side shoots should be allowed to grow to about 2 ft when they, too, are pinched out.

From the next winter on, pruning follows the same lines. Before the end of the year, prune all laterals back to two buds from the main stem. In spring, you have to start disbudding the laterals, to leave one every 12–15 inches along each side of the rod (the name given to the mature main stem). All others are rubbed out. Before long, each remaining lateral should produce a bunch of flowers, and it is then pinched out two leaves beyond. Laterals that don't produce flowers are left to grow on to 2 feet before being stopped. If sub-laterals appear, stop these at the first leaf.

When the leaves fall again, all laterals are again pruned back to one or two buds (the extra bud is an insurance policy but, with experience, you may find one bud is sufficient).

Outdoor vines: In a fine warm summer, a good outdoor crop can often be had from a suitable vine variety, such as Brandt (black) or Royal Muscadine (amber) grown against a wall. Pruning is similar to that for glass-house vines, except that subsidiary rods may be trained off the main one where space allows.

If an open site is chosen, it should face south and be sheltered from cold winds. The vines can be grown as

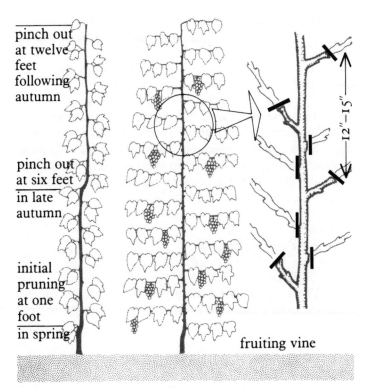

pinch out
at twelve
feet
following
autumn

pinch out
at six feet
in late
autumn

initial
pruning
at one
foot
in spring

12″–15″

fruiting vine

The stages of pruning a vine under glass

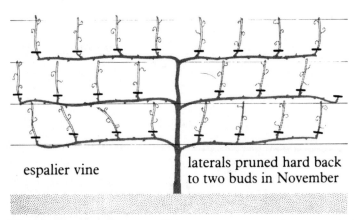

espalier vine

laterals pruned hard back
to two buds in November

Vine trained against a wall

75

cordons—treating the laterals as for glasshouse-grown vines—or as espaliers, with rods trained out each side of the main stem at vertical intervals of about 15 inches. Select laterals on the upper side only, spaced 18 inches apart, and treat them as for other forms.

A popular method is to train in three rods, one on each side, one vertically. This central rod is pruned to three buds, to produce three shoots. When the original two "arms" have fruited, they are pruned back to their replacement shoots, and the third is pruned to three buds to create the following season's replacements. The procedure is repeated year after year.

LOGANBERRIES
See Blackberries.

RASPBERRIES
There are two kinds of raspberries: summer-fruiting varieties, which are most commonly grown, and autumn-

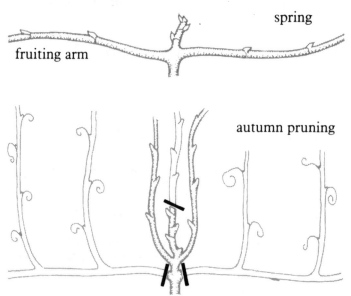

spring

fruiting arm

autumn pruning

Outdoor vine: a well-tried method

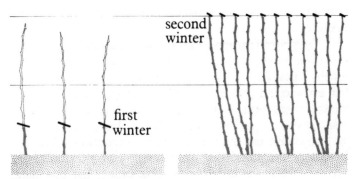

How to start raspberries

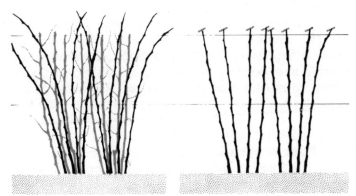

before pruning   (third winter)   after pruning

Cut out old canes, tie in the new

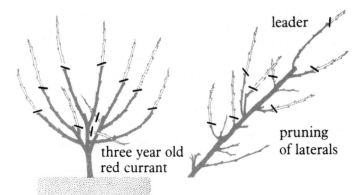

Redcurrants need spur-pruning

fruiting varieties. You must know which you have, for the pruning is different.

Summer-fruiting: Plant 15–18 inches apart, with 5–6 ft between the rows, which should run north and south. Then cut the canes back to 12 inches. New shoots will grow during the ensuing summer and these will fruit the following year. Remove any weak canes and tie in the rest, about 4 inches apart. The subsequent pruning pattern is regular: cut the old canes to ground level (don't leave any snags) as soon as possible after fruiting ends, and tie in the strongest of the new canes, but not more than 4 or 5 from each stool. In early spring, these should be tipped at a convenient height.

Autumn-fruiting: Initial cultivation is the same, but the pruning differs because, with these varieties (such as September), the fruit is produced on canes that emerge and develop the same year. So cut all canes almost to ground level in late winter. Support is rarely needed, since these raspberries grow to only about 4 ft.

RED and WHITE CURRANTS

Plant new bushes (usually two years old) 5–6 ft apart, cordons 15 inches apart. Initial pruning is the same as for gooseberries: cut the stems back by half to a good outward-facing bud, removing any weak growth. The annual extension growth of the leaders is cut back by about a half (depending on vigour) each winter and laterals are shortened to one inch or even less. This is because the fruit is borne on spurs at the base of the side shoots. Ripening of the new wood, and, of course, the fruit itself is helped if the laterals are summer-pruned— shortened to about five leaves soon after mid-summer. Redcurrants, like gooseberries, should always be grown on a leg, and the centre of the bushes kept well open.

CHAPTER NINE

Shrubs and Climbers – an Alphabetical List

ABELIA *chinensis*

Enjoys a sunny, sheltered position. Cut out an old branch occasionally to encourage young replacement growth from the base. Not quite hardy, and a hard winter may damage shoots. Leave any pruning till spring then cut back to healthy wood.

ABUTILON *vitifolium*

Tender, and in Britain can be grown outdoors only in mild districts, then best against a south wall. Little pruning needed, except for shape or to remove frost-damaged wood. Cut off faded flowers to save seed production.

ACACIA *dealbata*

Succeeds outdoors only in milder districts of Britain. Leave unpruned, apart from removal of dead or damaged

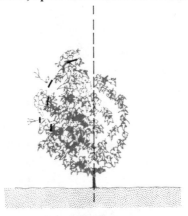

Abutilon

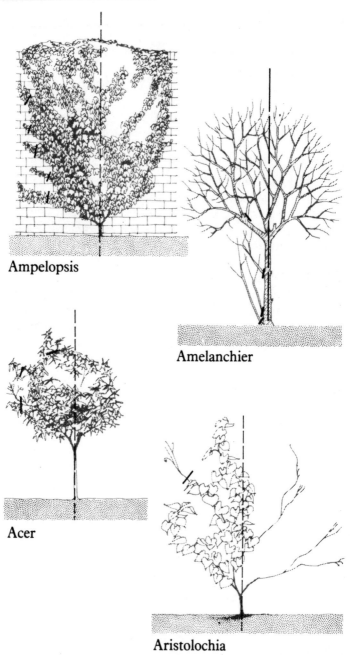

Ampelopsis

Amelanchier

Acer

Aristolochia

80

wood, until size necessitates some cutting back, which it will not resent. Do this in late spring.

ACER *palmatum*
The Japanese maples, needing lime-free soil, form naturally beautiful shapes with their delicate branches. Leave them to grow at will, removing only any dead wood in summer, or unwanted branches in late winter.

AMELANCHIER shrubby species
Keep this subject to a single stem, removing side branches up to a height of 5 ft and cutting out strong shoots thrown up from the base. Thin weak or over-crowding branches after flowering in late spring. Has fine autumn colouring.

AMPELOPSIS
A strong-growing climber, normally needing no pruning. But, if necessary, trim back in mid-winter.

ARALIA *elata*
This handsome shrub grows freely in well-drained soil and its natural, rather twisting branching habit should not be hindered. Remove any suckers unless you wish to extend the shrub's spread.

ARBUTUS
The evergreen Strawberry Tree (the fruit resembles strawberries) should be allowed to develop naturally. Restrict pruning to the removal of dead, straggling, or overcrowding wood in spring. Will submit to hard heading back if the tree gets too big.

ARISTOLOCHIA Dutchman's Pipe
This vigorous climber prefers a warm site. Any thinning of unwanted growths or dead wood should be done in early spring.

ARTEMISIA *arborescens, abrotanum* *Illustration p. 83*
Cut these shrubby plants back in spring, as soon as

81

new growth is seen. Otherwise straggling, untidy plants with bare stems will result.

ARUNDINARIA

The Bamboos can look after themselves. Cut old canes for stakes, right close to the ground, for the stumps are very sharp. Leave a few canes to support the younger growth.

AUCUBA *japonica*

Use secateurs, not shears, to prune this popular evergreen: if the leaves are cut across the edges will turn brown. Any hard cutting back should be done in spring and, if extensive, spread over two years.

AZALEA see also Rhododendron

No pruning is needed, except to remove dead, damaged or worn-out wood. Snap off faded blooms.

BAMBOO

See Arundinaria.

BERBERIS

Deciduous species are best pruned during the growing season when dead stems can be recognised and removed. Cut back to a strong outward or upward-growing lateral.

Evergreen species should be pruned after flowering.

BIGNONIA *capreolata*

This vigorous climber needs a warm wall in a mild district. Space out the main stems evenly, tying them in to supports. Prune strong laterals in spring by a third to a half, and cut out old or weak ones.

BUDDLEIA *Davidii*

—The one with the long, tapering mauve or purple flowers—must be cut back in late winter or early spring to leave only one or two buds at the base of the previous season's growth. These will grow several feet long in one summer. The woody prunings make useful stakes.

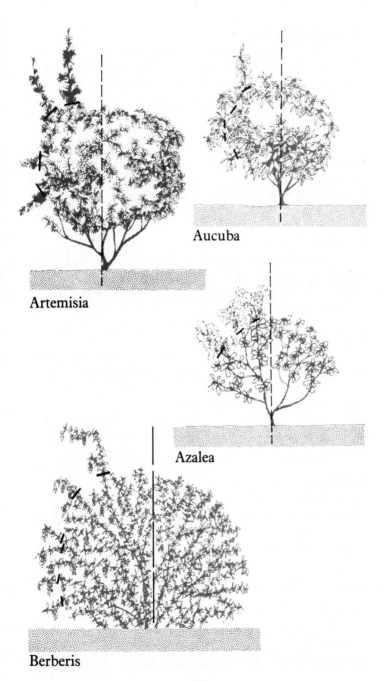

Artemisia

Aucuba

Azalea

Berberis

83

BUDDLEIA *globosa*

Cut out weak or damaged wood in early spring, but otherwise do not prune, for it flowers at the ends of the previous year's growths. A too-large shrub may be cut back hard in spring, losing that year's flowers.

BUDDLEIA *alternifolia*

Cut back the arching stems as soon as the flowers fade to strong young replacement shoots. Remove all dead wood, of which much occurs each year. Young plants should be trained to form a standard on a 3–4 ft leg.

BUXUS

The Common Box—much used for low hedges or edging—responds well to regular trimming (best in spring and late summer). No special care is needed unless one indulges in topiary.

CALLICARPA

The only pruning needed is to cut out any dead, damaged or overcrowding growth in spring.

CALLISTEMON Bottle-brush

Tender and needs a warm wall in Britain. Little pruning is necessary: any unwanted growth should be removed after flowering.

CALLUNA *vulgaris*

These heathers are summer flowering and bloom on the current season's shoots. In spring prune the previous year's growth (*not* the whole plant) by half to preserve a bushy habit. Beware of cutting back into old, bare wood: it rarely breaks into new growth. With dwarfer forms shears or an electric trimmer may be used.

CAMELLIA

This lovely shrub is best left unpruned while growing well except for the removal of any dead or straggling branches, or frosted tips in spring. Old,

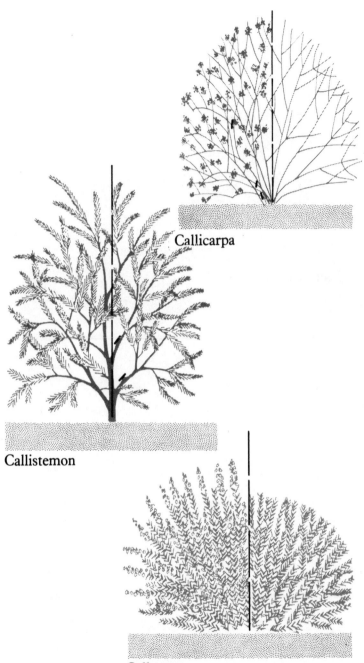

Callicarpa

Callistemon

Calluna

85

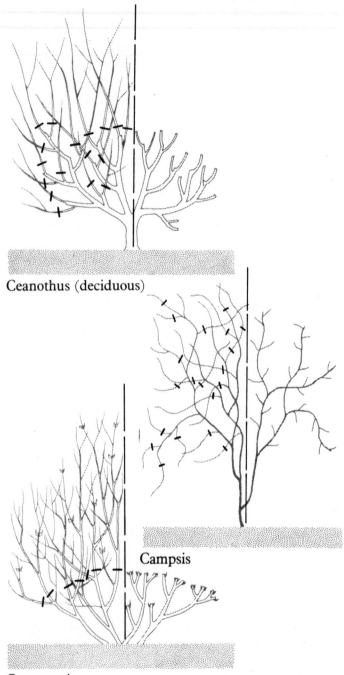

Ceanothus (deciduous)

Campsis

Caryopteris

86

weakening subjects can sometimes be given a new lease of life by hard cutting back, compensated for by generous feeding with organic matter, especially leaf mould. Regular removal of the faded blooms helps the appearance of the shrubs during the flowering period.

CAMPSIS

This climber, needing full sun, flowers in the second half of summer on the current season's growth. Prune the previous year's shoots to two or three buds in early spring, unless a shoot is needed for extension or replacement. Such shoots should be pruned back by a third to a half.

CARYOPTERIS *clandonensis*

This blue-flowered shrub blooms in late summer on the current season's growth. Cut the thin branches back to within an inch or two of the older wood in spring. Larger bushes can be formed with slightly less hard pruning, but the flower heads, though numerous, will be smaller.

CEANOTHUS

Evergreen species are usually grown against a south or west wall for protection, with the leading stems tied in fan-wise. Prune laterals to two or three buds after flowering (in spring), but keep a few unpruned for replacement, so that the shrub is always well furnished with new growth.

Deciduous kinds, such as Gloire de Versailles, are late summer flowering, and are usually grown as bushes. Prune the previous year's growth back to two or three pairs of buds in spring, and cut out any weak growth. C. *Burkwoodii* is similarly pruned.

CERATOSTIGMA

Prefers full sun, and may need a warm wall. It flowers in autumn on the same season's growth, so prune the previous year's stems close to their base in spring, unless already cut to the ground by frost.

CHAENOMELES Japanese Quince

Popularly known as "Japonica" (one of the species). Grown as a bush, one or two older stems may be cut to the ground each year. Side shoots should be shortened to two or three buds after flowering. When grown against a wall, summer-prune the laterals to six inches and further prune back to one or two buds in winter.

CHAMAECYPARIS

Most often grown are the forms and species of *Lawsoniana*. Bushes need little or no pruning. To form a hedge, allow the young plants to reach a little more than the required height, then trim off six inches of the leading stems to promote lateral growth and the formation of a firm top, which should always be kept narrower than the base.

CHIMONANTHUS *praecox* Winter Sweet

Allow this scented, winter-flowering shrub to develop naturally: When mature, confine pruning to the removal of any old or weakening branches, allowing younger growths to take their place. When grown against a wall, shorten laterals immediately after flowering to two or three buds.

CHOISYA *ternata*

This sweetly scented shrub flowers in late spring and early summer and prefers a warm, sheltered site. It may be left unpruned, except to shape, but if the faded flowered stems are cut back to about 9 inches a second flowering usually results.

CISTUS Sun Rose or Rock Rose

These dwarf shrubs should not be hard pruned. Merely clip them over after flowering. Old plants that become straggling are best replaced by plants from seed or cuttings.

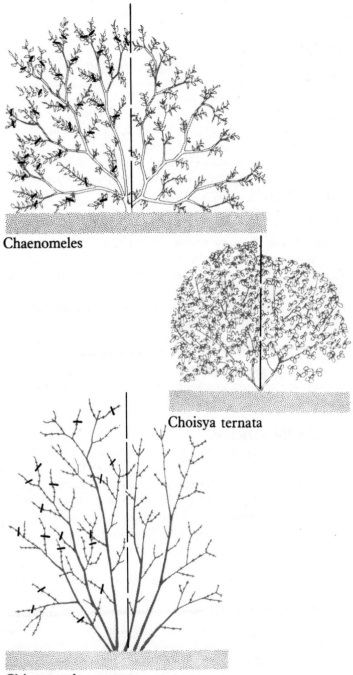

Chaenomeles

Choisya ternata

Chimonanthus praecox

89

CLEMATIS

This splendid, self-clinging climber divides into two main groups:-

1. Those that flower mainly in the first half of summer on growth made the previous year. These include the *florida* and *patens* groups, with varieties such as Duchess of Edinburgh, Lasurstern and Nelly Moser.

When the flowers fade, cut them off to strong buds just below. In winter, train out the main branches to prevent their becoming a tangled mass.

2. Those that flower in the second half of summer on growth made the same season. Included are the *lanuginosa*, *jackmanii* and *viticella* groups, with varieties such as Comtesse de Bouchaud, Jackmanii, Hagley Hybrid, and Ville de Lyon.

Cut all the previous year's growth down to a strong pair of buds near the base in late winter.

The species *flammula* and *tangutica* are cut back to about 3 ft. The very vigorous spring-flowering *montana* is either left to grow at will, or—while still young—its main shoots are trained out wide, and the side branches are pruned almost to their base in late summer.

CLERODENDRUM

The species *trichotomum* is a strong-growing shrub with scented, verbena-like flowers borne on shoots ripened the previous year. Shorten these in late spring to the nearest pair of good buds. Bright blue berries form in autumn. C. *bungei*, a suckering shrub, should be cut back hard to healthy wood in late spring.

CORNUS

The tall-growing flowering species, such as *florida*, *kousa*, and *mas*, need no regular pruning. Those dog-woods grown for the beauty of their highly coloured stems (*alba, sanguinea*, etc.) should be cut close to the ground in spring. Alternatively they can be so pruned every other spring; or—a compromise—half the one-year-old stems can be pruned hard, and the other half left

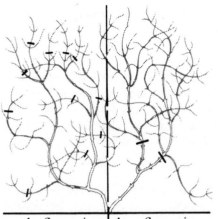

early flowering | late flowering

Clematis

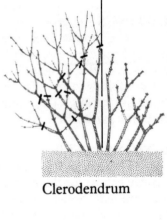

Clerodendrum

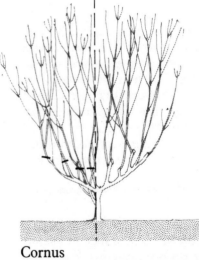

Cornus

91

to keep the shrub furnished, these being cut to the ground the following spring.

CORONILLA Crown Vetch

Free-flowering if grown in a warm, sheltered position. Little regular pruning is needed, beyond the removal of the odd older stem in early spring. The evergreen C. *glauca*, best grown against a warm wall, may be lightly pruned after flowering.

CORYLOPSIS

This beautiful shrub carries its scented flowers in drooping racemes on leafless shoots in spring. No regular pruning is needed, but older branches may be removed, or cut back to replacement shoots, after flowering.

COTINUS *coggyria*

The Smoke Tree, sometimes know as *rhus cotinus*, is best left unpruned, especially if the smoky inflorescences are valued. But if the accent is to be on the rich, reddish-purple foliage, the young wood may be cut down to two buds in spring. The forms Flame and Royal Purple respond particularly well to this treatment.

COTONEASTER

There is a wide range of species, all hardy, and mainly grown for the brilliant colours of their berries and autumn leaf. Some are deciduous, some evergreen. The tallest make small trees: others, such as *horizontalis*, are of spreading habit and will cover either wall or bank. Most are best left unpruned, except for the removal of an unwanted branch. Old, untidy bushes may be pruned hard—deciduous kinds in early spring, evergreen in later spring. Hedging forms can be clipped between late spring and late summer.

CRATAEGUS

The hawthorns need no pruning except for the occasional removal of an overcrowding branch in winter. The lower branches may be pruned away if a tree with a short trunk is required. The thorns make excellent and impenetrable hedges: clip them in summer as necessary.

CUPRESSOCYPARIS

Leylandii has gained popularity because of its rapid growth habit, often putting on three feet a year. It can be allowed to grow into a tall graceful tree, but if needed as a screen or a hedge, it can be cut and maintained at the required height.

CUPRESSUS

These conifers, not so hardy as the chamaecyparis species, are nearly all neatly conical or columnar and rarely need pruning. C. *macrocarpa* succeeds as a hedge in mild or maritime districts, but any hard cutting back often proves fatal.

CYTISUS

Most of the brooms should be pruned as soon as the flowers fade, usually by shortening the young flowering shoots by about two-thirds. Do not cut into the old wood, which is unlikely to "break". C. *battandieri* (usually grown as a wall shrub): Restrict pruning to the removal in winter of the oldest wood, or unwanted or straggling shoots. Tie in young growths in late summer.

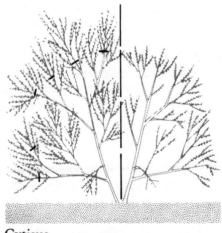

Cytisus

93

DABOECIA

This heath, forming a dwarf shrub, bears large, showy flowers over a long period in summer. Prune the old flowered shoots in early spring to newer growth lower down.

DAPHNE

The species *mezereum*, sweetly scented and flowering on bare branches in early spring, is of neat habit, as long as it is grown in an open position, and needs no pruning. D. *odora* is wider spreading, and may require light trimming after flowering. Treat D. *cneorum* in the same way.

DEUTZIA

This shrub flowers in early summer on growth made the previous year, so prune back to young replacement shoots after flowering ends. New stems spring freely from the ground and some of these should be preserved, but not all, or you will have an unmanageable thicket and few flowers. To balance the new stems, cut the oldest to the ground each year.

DIERVILLA

A small shrub producing a number of suckers. Remove some of the older stems in early spring. Any straggling branches may be pruned back after flowering.

ECCREMOCARPUS *scaber*

This vigorous, self-clinging climber needs a sheltered site and may suffer badly in a hard winter. Prune in late winter, cutting out dead stems and pruning other growth back to healthy wood.

ELAEAGNUS

Deciduous kinds, such as E. *angustifolia*, may be pruned hard in late winter. E. *pungens* and other evergreen forms need little pruning except to restrict size. Any branches of variegated types showing a tendency to revert should be cut out. The long rambling growths

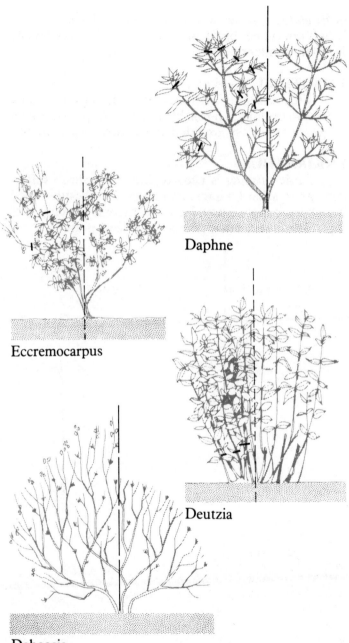

Daphne

Eccremocarpus

Deutzia

Daboecia

95

of E. *glabra* may be cut back in autumn. E. *ebbingei* can be left unpruned, but if any cutting back is necessary, do it in late summer.

EMBOTHRIUM *coccineum*
The Chilean Fire Bush succeeds only in milder areas. No pruning is normally needed, except to maintain shape, or to remove growth damaged after a hard winter.

ENKIANTHUS
Little pruning is needed. But if the shrub suffers damage in a hard winter, cutting back to healthy wood may be required. Should growth become straggly over the years, it will usually respond to hard pruning.

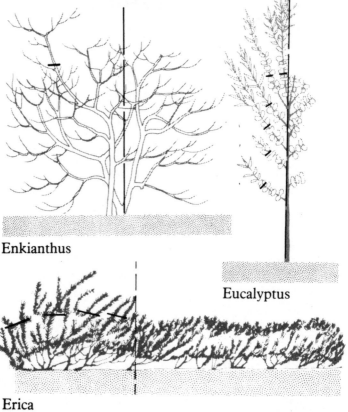

Enkianthus

Eucalyptus

Erica

96

ERICA Heather

All heathers should be pruned back after flowering, but avoid cutting into old, bare wood, which rarely breaks into new growth (*arborea*, the Tree Heath, is an exception). In their early years, heathers should be pruned with a sharp knife or secateurs, but later shears or an electric pruner will speed the work.

ESCALLONIA

This free-flowering, small-leafed shrub prefers a mild climate and is particularly successful near the sea. It can be grown as a specimen, screen, or hedge. Any pruning should be carried out immediately flowering ends: this includes trimming if a hedge. If hard cutting back is called for, it will normally break from old wood.

EUCALYPTUS

Most species rapidly grow into trees unless pruned regularly. E. *gunnii*, one of the hardiest, will lose the attractive coin-shaped blue-grey foliage, so well liked by flower arrangers, unless the branches are pruned back hard annually in spring. Tub-grown plants should be cut almost to soil level each year.

EUCRYPHIA

These delightful shrubs do not like being pruned, so allow them to grow naturally except to remove any dead or damaged wood. This is best done in spring.

EUONYMUS

Among the best evergreens for town or seaside use. E. *japonicus* (there are many fine variegated forms) and E. *fortunei radicans* make excellent hedges. Prune in spring, pruning each individual branch rather than clipping with shears, which damages the leaves. Deciduous species rarely need pruning.

FATSHEDERA *lizei*   *Illustration p. 99*

This large-leafed shrub prefers a shady site and makes good ground cover with its spreading habit. If strong upright growths appear, prune these down in summer to induce the production of side shoots.

FATSIA *japonica*
This exotic looking shrub also prefers full shade, but will tolerate semi-shade. Straggling branches can be cut back to near ground level in spring.

FICUS *carica* (Fig)
This subject makes a very big shrub or spreading tree, and does well against a wall. Size can be limited— and fruiting encouraged—by limiting its root spread (method: plant in an old tank, or other container, let into the ground). Encourage the more upright, rather than horizontal growths.

FORSYTHIA
Cut back the flowered shoots as soon as the florets drop, to strong new shoots. Remove a few complete older branches to make room for vigorous growth arising from the base. If F. *suspensa* gets out of hand, it can be cut almost to the ground. F. *intermedia spectabilis* makes a good hedge and can be clipped formally in mid-summer without loss of flower.

FOTHERGILLA
This needs little pruning except to cut out an occasional old branch in winter. The twiggy growths springing from the base carry flowers in spring, so do not prune them.

FREMONTIA *californica*
Slightly tender in Britain, and best grown against a warm wall. Little pruning needed, except to cut back laterals growing outwards.

FUCHSIA
Hardy species, such as *megallanica* and *riccartonii*, will often be cut to the ground in winter but in mild districts the top growth should be pruned well down to

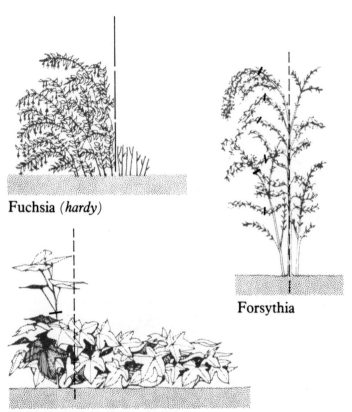

Fuchsia *(hardy)*

Forsythia

Fatshedera lizei

Ficus carica

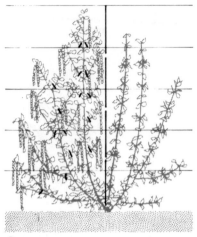

Garrya

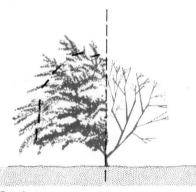

Genista

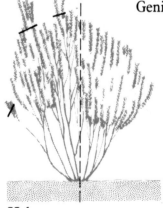

Hebe

100

living wood (test: if the bark is scratched and shows green, the stem is alive). Side shoots may be pruned back by a half to two-thirds.

GARRYA *elliptica*
When grown as a shrub, prune only to restrict size and spread, after flowering. When grown against a wall the previous year's growth should be shortened almost back to the framework of stems in late spring.

GENISTA
Prune much in the same way as cytisus. Shorten stems of G. *cinerea* after flowering, back to replacement shoots. Clip G. *hispanica* (Spanish Broom) lightly after flowering, and remove any dead or aging wood. It does not pay to cut back hard into the old wood.

GREVILLEA
Prune in spring to keep the shrub shapely, to thin unwanted growth, or to cut back any frost-damaged wood.

GRISELINIA
A leafy evergreen needing little pruning except to maintain shape. When grown as a hedge it may be trimmed in early summer.

HAMAMELIS Wych Hazel
This winter-flowering shrub or small tree can be left to grow at will, but if there are any unwanted branches, remove these in spring. Remove suckers as they appear.

HEBE
The shrubby veronicas may be cut back by frost in winter, but usually make good growth from the old wood. So—whether frosted or not—trim back to healthy shoots in spring.

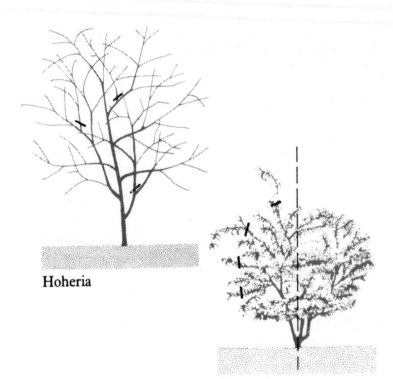

Hoheria

Hippophae

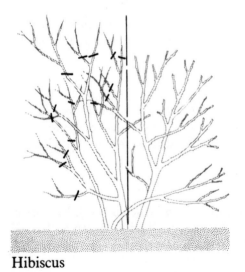

Hibiscus

HEDERA Ivy

All ivies are best left to grow freely where there is room, but do not resent being cut back hard. Spring is the best time to prune, and wall-grown ivies can be clipped over then, and again, if necessary in July.

HIBISCUS

H. *syriacus*, the only species hardy enough to be commonly grown in Britain, flowers in late summer on the current season's growth. Prune either immediately after flowering or in spring, thinning out weak or dead wood, and keeping the shrub shapely. Tender species should be pruned in early spring.

HIPPOPHAE *rhamnoides*

The spiny Sea Buckthorn normally (and fortunately!) needs no pruning. But if any branches straggle cut these back in late winter to about 3 feet.

HOHERIA

It is only occasionally necessary to cut out one or two of the older branches, either completely or back to a replacement lateral. Evergreen species need be pruned only to restrict size and maintain shape. Do this in spring. Hoherias need a sheltered site.

HONEYSUCKLE

See Lonicera.

HYDRANGEA   *Illustration p. 105*

The popular *macrophylla* species (divided into the *hortensia* and Lacecap groups) flower on buds formed the previous season. Except in mild districts, the old flower heads should be left on over winter to protect these buds. In spring cut back each stem to a plump pair of buds, except the oldest, or weakest stems, which should be cut close to the ground.

To reduce the size of an over-large bush, cut half of the branches back almost to the ground in early spring, pruning the others lightly, as above. The next year it will be the turn of the remainder to be cut right down.

H. *paniculata* flowers on the current year's growth and should therefore be pruned hard, to the lowest pair of buds, or even to near ground level, in late winter or early spring. Thin out any weak or overcrowding stems.

H. *petiolaris*, a self-clinging climber, may need some pruning back in spring if it grows out too far from its wall or other support. Spread the work over two or three years to avoid too much loss of flower.

HYPERICUM

H. *patulum* flowers on the current year's growth and may be trimmed back in spring. Any old or weak wood should be cut to the base. Aim at encouraging as much young growth as possible.

H. *calycinum* (Rose of Sharon, St John's Wort) is used mainly as ground cover, or on banks, and should be cut back hard in early spring to keep it tidy. Shears or electric trimmers may be used.

HYSSOPUS

Prune back hard the previous summer's growth in early spring.

ILEX

Hollies are best pruned, if necessary, in late spring although, with female plants, this may result in the loss of some berries. Normally it is necessary only to shorten a branch here and there to preserve shape: but hollies will stand quite hard cutting back. Trim hedges between late spring and late summer.

JASMINUM *officinale* *Illustration p. 107*

The white, sweet-scented summer-flowering kind should be planted only where it can be given its head since pruning the tangle of branches and shoots is difficult. When cutting back does become necessary prune branches to replacement shoots well down in late summer.

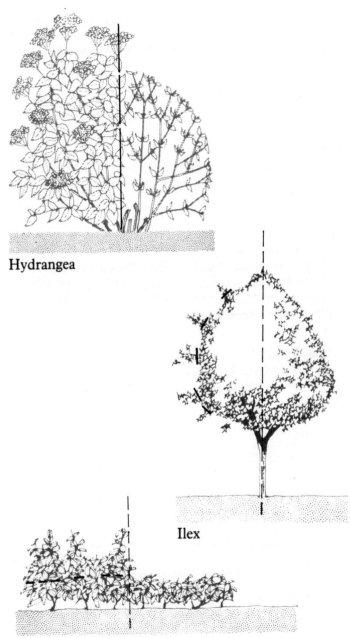

Hydrangea

Ilex

Hypericum *calycinum*

The yellow *nudiflorum*, flowering in winter on bare stems, must be pruned hard each spring unless much dead wood is to form. Shorten the flowered shoots back to within an inch or two of the older wood, and tie in any strong shoots needed as extensions.

The tender J. *polyanthum* should be pruned back moderately after flowering.

KALMIA

Little pruning is necessary, except to shorten any straggling growth after flowering. Remove the faded flower heads to prevent seeding.

KERRIA *japonica*

This popular spring-flowering shrub, known as Bachelor's Buttons, is constantly throwing up new shoots from the base, so—after flowering—cut a proportion of the stems almost to ground level and the rest well down to replacement shoots.

KOLKWITZIA

The arching branches are best left unpruned, but old and weak growth should be cut back in June after flowering.

LAUREL

See Prunus.

LAURUS *nobilis*

The Bay Laurel may be pruned carefully with secateurs in spring (random clipping with shears cuts the leaves, causing brown scars). The shrub will respond to hard cutting back if this becomes necessary.

LAVANDULA *Illustration p. 108*

If lavender is to be kept bushy and compact it must be clipped back every spring down to young shoots but never into the old wood. Left unpruned, the bushes soon

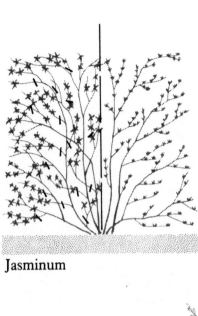

Jasminum

Kerria japonica

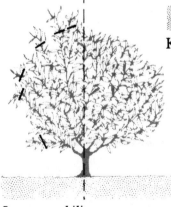

Laurus *nobilis*

107

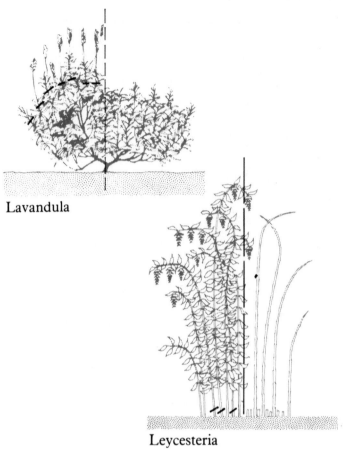

Lavandula

Leycesteria

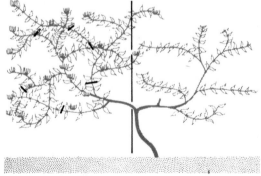

Lonicera periclymenum

become loose and straggling. Trim off the faded flower spikes in late summer.

LAVATERA
The Tree Mallow needs little pruning except to trim off any frosted shoots in spring, or to maintain shape.

LEPTOSPERMUM
Prune after flowering to keep the shrub shapely, and thin any overcrowding branches. Except in mild districts, it needs a warm wall.

LEYCESTERIA *formosa*
Strong new shoots break continually from the base, flowering the same year. A proportion of the older stems should therefore be cut back to the ground each spring. Alternatively, the whole bush can be cut to the base, but compensate with generous feeding.

LIGUSTRUM *See Privet for illustration*
The oval-leafed (L. *ovalifolium*), so commonly grown as a hedge, cheerfully responds to frequent clipping from spring to autumn. Neglected hedges can be cut back hard in spring. Cut back newly planted ones by half in spring. When grown in open situations, the only pruning necessary is to preserve shape.

LONICERA
The common honeysuckle (L. *periclymenum*) flowers on the previous summer's growth. So any pruning should be done as soon as the flowers fade, removing some of the flowered stems in favour of newly-forming ones.

The evergreen L. *japonica* flowers on the current season's growth. Clip it back hard with shears in early spring when grown against a wall.

The Chinese honeysuckle, L. *nitida*, popular as a hedge, needs trimming two or three times during the summer. The top must always be kept narrower than the base or the hedge will become top heavy and can collapse under the weight of snow. The hedge can be cut back hard in late spring if overgrown.

LUPINUS *arboreus*
The tree Lupin should be pruned in early spring, cutting out old wood and shortening younger growths almost to their base. Remove the faded flowers.

MAGNOLIA
It is rarely necessary to prune M. *soulangiana* except to remove damaged or unwanted branches in the second half of summer, when any bleeding will quickly heal. Paint large wounds with a sealant. M. *stellata* needs little pruning except for shape. M. *grandiflora*, a magnificent evergreen, is usually grown against a warm wall in Britain. Pruning is rarely necessary except to restrict its size: then treat as for *soulangiana*.

MAHONIA
M. *aquifolium* does not normally need pruning, but, if not grown for its ground covering qualities, its spreading growth can be restricted by cutting out suckers and pruning back the main branches after flowering.
M. *japonica*, the sweetly-scented *bealii* and the splendid hybrid Charity are best left unpruned.

MYRTUS
The myrtles need a mild climate, and in Britain the common myrtle (M. *communis*) is often grown against a wall, where it may be clipped over in spring. All the myrtles will usually break from the base if hard cutting back is necessary.

NERIUM Oleander
This lovely evergreen shrub is tender, but can be grown in Britain in tubs which are stood in a sunny place in summer and given frost-free protection in winter. Prune after flowering to maintain shape.

110

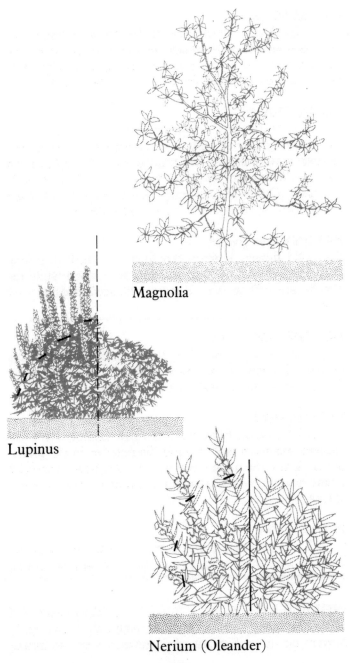

Magnolia

Lupinus

Nerium (Oleander)

111

OLEARIA *haastii*

The Daisy Bush may be left to grow freely but responds well to cutting back for size or shape. It may be damaged by frost, so do not prune till shoots begin to break in spring, when any damage can be assessed.

OSMANTHUS

The fragrant O. *delavayi* flowers in spring, so do any pruning immediately after flowering. When grown against a wall it may be pruned back to replacement shoots. When grown as a hedge, trim before mid-summer. Other species may be cut back hard when overgrown, or to preserve shape and balance.

PAEONY tree species

Old flowered stems should be cut back to plump buds in early spring. Cut out any dead wood while the shrubs are still in leaf. Remove the seed pods as they form.

PARTHENOCISSUS

This genus includes the self-clinging Virginia creeper. Do any cutting back in winter: only the young shoots can attach to wall or other support.

PASSIFLORA

The Passion Flower is a rampant climber, and will succeed against a wall in mild districts: or in the greenhouse. Train the main stems out in a rough fan shape and prune laterals back to strong buds near the base in early spring.

PERNETTYA

Little pruning is necessary except to curb suckers. Cut out old or worn out branches, and any straggling growths in April.

PHILADELPHUS   *Illustration p. 115*

The Mock Orange (often wrongly called "syringa") flowers on growth made the previous year, so prune

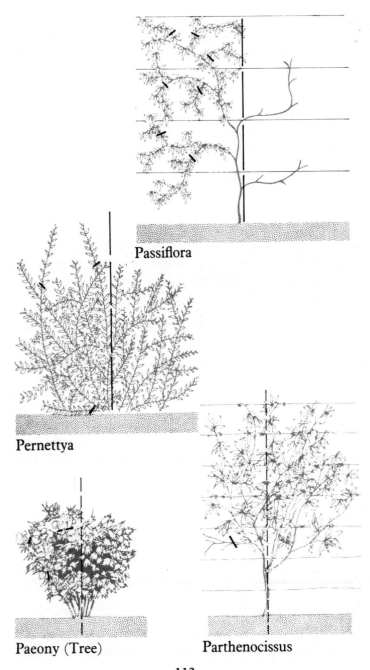

Passiflora

Pernettya

Paeony (Tree)

Parthenocissus

113

immediately after flowering. Cut back to strong new shoots and remove weak and overcrowding growth. Each year remove one or more of the oldest branches to encourage a continuous supply of young wood from the base.

PHLOMIS
Cut back any shoots damaged by frost, or straggling stems, in spring. It will respond to any hard cutting back necessary.

PHOTINIA
Young growths of some deciduous varieties, such as Red Robin and Robusta, have brilliant red young leaves in spring. Other species have fine autumn colouring. If any pruning is necessary, winter is best for deciduous kinds, spring for evergreen.

PIERIS
Any pruning should normally be confined to the removal of wood damaged in a hard winter, or—also in spring—to preserve shape. The shrubs usually break well from old wood.

PITTOSPORUM
This shrub does best in mild districts, especially by the sea. Any pruning for shape or to cut out damaged wood should be carried out in spring. It breaks well from old wood.

POLYGONUM *baldschuanicum*
The rampant Russian Vine is best given plenty of room to grow as it pleases. But if pruning becomes essential, wait till after leaf fall when the branch system can be clearly seen. Remember that the harder you prune, the more vigorous will be the subsequent growth.

POTENTILLA
The shrubby potentillas should be pruned in spring, removing any weak growth and shortening the strong

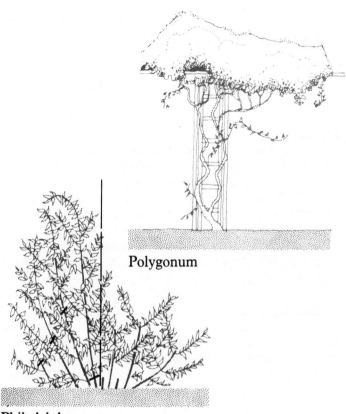

Polygonum

Philadelphus

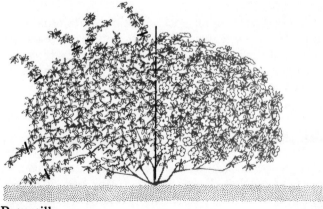

Potentilla

115

stems by a third to a half. Any overall clipping will produce a mass of twiggy growth and fewer flowers.

PRIVET
See illustration opposite and Ligustrum for description.

PRUNUS
The ornamental members of this very large genus are, on the whole, best left unpruned. If any cutting is necessary, do it after flowering ends.

P. *laurocerasus* (the Cherry Laurel) and *lusitanica* (the Portugal Laurel) should be pruned in the same way as the bay laurel (see Laurus *nobilis*).

P. *triloba* flowers best if the young branches are cut back hard after flowering, to within two or three buds of the older wood.

PUNICA *granatum*
The Pomegranate needs a warm wall in southern Britain to succeed, and an exceptional summer to make fruit. Cut out some of the older and weaker wood in late spring. If grown against a wall spur back shoots growing outwards. Prune older branches back to replacement shoots as necessary in late winter.

PYRACANTHA
When grown in an open situation, little pruning is needed. When used as a wall shrub, only those branches growing outwards need be pruned back, preferably after flowering in early summer. Any extensive clipping back will result in loss of flowers and, more important, the rich orange or scarlet berries.

RHODODENDRON
In general, this large family which includes azaleas needs little pruning beyond the removal of dead wood or unwanted branches. If any severe cutting back is necessary, carry it out over two or three years, always after the flowering period.

116

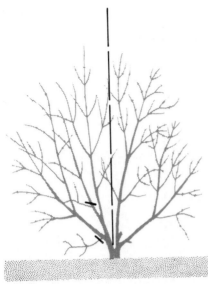

Punica

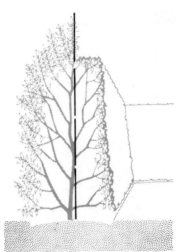

Privet

Pyracantha

117

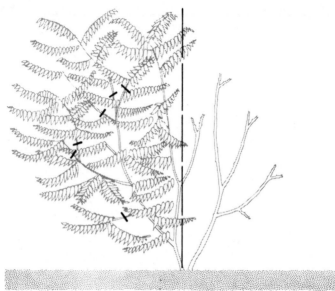

Rhus *typhina*

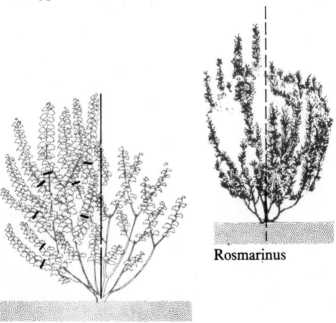

Ribes

Rosmarinus

118

When possible, the faded flower trusses should be snapped off. Remove suckers from grafted plants.

RHUS

The Sumachs need little pruning. Shrubby kinds should be allowed to branch naturally. Younger stems thrown up from the base can replace old, outworn branches.

R. *typhina* can be cut back in spring to two or three buds of the older wood.

RIBES *sanguineum*

For best results, the Flowering Currant should be pruned immediately after flowering, cutting the flowered stems down to good replacement shoots. Cut a portion of the old branches to the ground each year, so that the shrub is always well furnished with young wood.

ROMNEYA

The top growth of this sub-shrub is often cut to the ground in winter. But this does not matter, since it flowers on the current year's growth. If some stems remain undamaged, cut down to good buds in spring.

ROSES

See Chapter Five.

ROSMARINUS

Rosemary (R. *officinalis*) should be pruned back moderately each spring to prevent its becoming loose and straggling. Old, untidy plants are best replaced. Informal hedge should be lightly pruned after flowering.

RUTA *graveolens*

A sub-shrub, it should be cut back hard in spring to produce the shapely blue-green mound of foliage so much admired.

SALIX

Those forms of willow (such as S. *alba vitellina*)

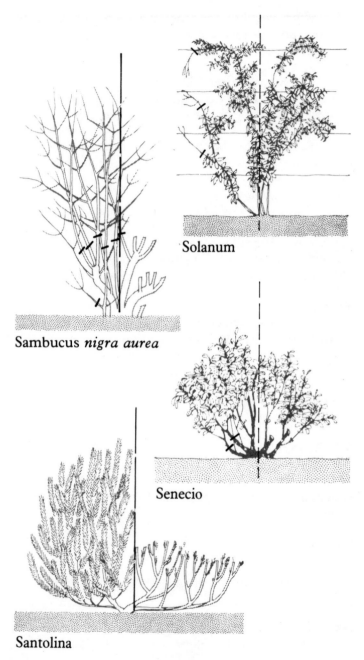

Solanum

Sambucus *nigra aurea*

Senecio

Santolina

grown for their coloured stems should be cut down almost to the ground in spring. Alternatively, cut half down one year, half the next.

SAMBUCUS

Cut out some of the older wood in winter—severely if the bush has got out of hand. Young shoots generally come readily from the base. S. *nigra aurea*, grown for its golden foliage, should be cut back hard in early spring.

SANTOLINA

Young plants are best trimmed back in autumn. As soon as the bush begins to make so much growth that the branches spread, it should be cut back in spring, close to the old wood.

SARCOCOCCA

This small evergreen suckering shrub bearing fragrant white flowers in winter, needs little or no pruning, except to cut out any old, outworn branch in spring.

SENECIO

S. *greyi* and S. *laxifolius* need regular moderate pruning in spring, as new growth begins, to keep the bushes reasonably compact. But cut back hard if growth has begun to sprawl.

SKIMMIA

The habit is compact. Should any pruning be necessary, do it in spring.

SOLANUM

The two climbing members of the potato faimly, S. *crispum* and S. *jasminoides*, need a warm, sheltered site Cut out weak or unwanted wood in early spring, back to replacement growths. These should be tied in when the shrub is grown against a wall or other support.

SPARTIUM *junceum*

When the bush is young, prune the stems back by half each spring. As it matures, shoots formed the previous summer should be cut back hard, close to—but not into—the older wood.

SPIRAEA

Species flowering on the previous year's wood (such as *arguta*, *henryi*, *thunbergii* are pruned after flowering, back to good replacement shoots, but occasionally close to the ground. Keep the emphasis on the continual production of new wood.

Species flowering on the current season's wood (such as *bumalda* and *japonica*) should be pruned hard in early spring, the older growth to the ground, younger wood by a third to a half. S. *bumalda* Anthony Waterer, however, should be cut almost to the ground in early spring.

STEPHANANDRA

Cut faded flowered shoots back after flowering to good replacement shoots or—in some cases—to ground level. The aim is to encourage the production of strong stems from the base. The emphasis is on foliage rather than flowers.

STRANVAESIA

Little pruning is needed, except for the occasional removal of old wood, back to suitable replacement growth, in spring.

SYMPHORICARPOS

The ample production of suckers quickly turns the Snowberry (S. *albus*) into a thicket, and there is little point in trying to alter its natural habit. Cut out dead wood as it appears and a few of the older stems each year.

SYRINGA Lilac   *Illustration p. 125*

Any pruning beyond the removal of the faded flower heads (where these can be reached) will result in

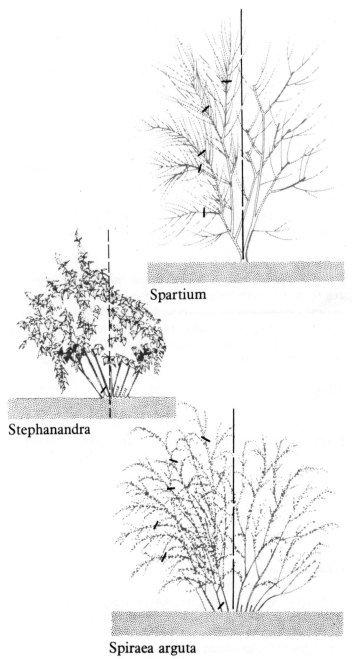

Spartium

Stephanandra

Spiraea arguta

123

some loss of bloom the next year. This is because lilacs flower mainly on shoots produced close beneath the old flower spike.

The odd unwanted branch may be cut out after flowering, but any severe pruning to regulate size or improve shape should be done in the dormant season. Remove all suckers as soon as they are seen.

TAMARIX *pentandra*

Left to itself, this delightful seaside shrub—used to fierce winds and poor, sandy soil—can become large and top-heavy when grown in the shelter of a garden. So prune last year's shoots back to within two or three buds of the older wood each spring.

TAXUS *baccata* Yew

When forming a hedge, allow the leading stems to reach the required height before pruning them. Trimming is best carried out in the second half of summer, but late spring is acceptable, and any hard pruning should be done at this time. Individual specimens should be allowed to develop naturally.

THUJA *plicata*

A fine evergreen hedging plant. Allow the leader to grow a few inches above the desired height before pruning to 6 inches below it. Subsequent growth is trimmed at the required height in late spring and/or late summer.

TSUGA

T. *heterophylla* makes a useful hedge and should be treated like thuja.

ULEX

Gorse needs no pruning until it becomes straggling with age. To avoid complete loss of bloom, cut back half the branches to within a foot or so of the ground after spring flowering; the other half one to two years later. New growth will spring freely from old wood.

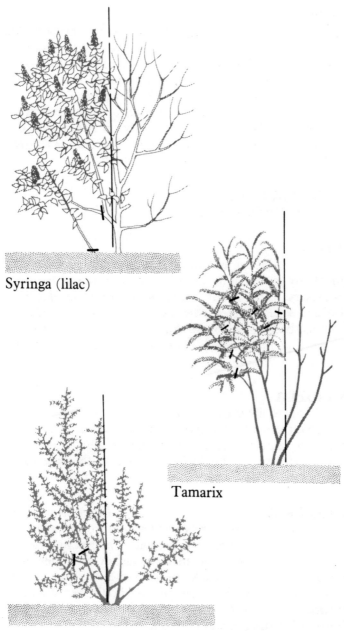

Syringa (lilac)

Tamarix

Ulex

125

VIBURNUM

Most species continually push up new growth from the base. These should be used to replace old, weakening branches which can be removed in winter. Pruning to restrict size or maintain shape, by cutting back to strong new shoots, should be done after flowering.

V. *tinus*, one of the winter-flowering evergreen species, can be pruned, if necessary, in late spring. Cut back overgrown bushes as hard as you like, since they invariably break freely into new growth.

VIRGINIA CREEPER

See Parthenocissus.

VITIS

V. *coignetiae* and other vigorous species may be left to climb and ramble at will. But if pruning becomes necessary, carry it out in mid-winter to avoid bleeding. Foliage vines trained over pergolas or walls should be spurred back to one or two buds in winter, as for fruiting vines. Laterals may be summer-pruned to about five leaves.

WEIGELA

This easily grown summer-flowering shrub blooms on lateral growths formed the previous year. So prune back to suitable replacement shoots after flowering. Some older wood should be cut to near the base each year.

WISTERIA   *Illustration p. 128*

This beautiful climber is usually grown against a wall, or over a verandah or pergola. The leading shoots are tied in to form the main branches and then the laterals are spurred back in the same way as trained apples and pears. The new shoots should be summer-pruned to about 6 inches after flowering ends, and shortened further in winter to one or two buds. Wisterias can also be grown as large bushes, the main growths

126

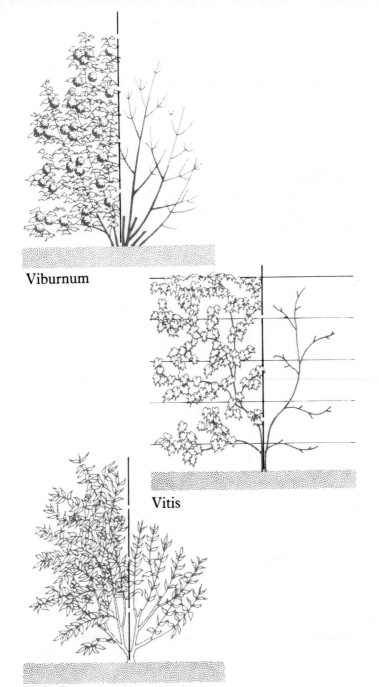

Viburnum

Vitis

Weigela

being supported on stout stakes or other framework. Pruning is similar to that for the climber.

YUCCA
Simply remove dead leaves in spring and faded flower stems in autumn.

ZENOBIA
Pruning can be confined to the occasional removal of an old branch, and the pruning back to replacement shoots of faded flower stems when dead-heading in summer.

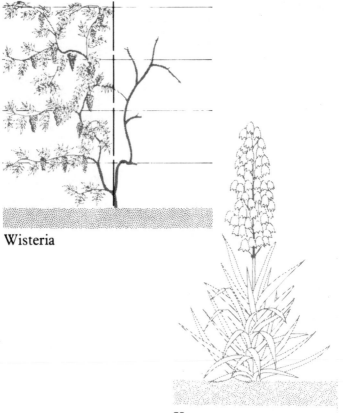

Wisteria

Yucca